STS

Exam Secrets
Study Guide

DEAR FUTURE EXAM SUCCESS STORY

First of all, **THANK YOU** for purchasing Mometrix study materials!

Second, congratulations! You are one of the few determined test-takers who are committed to doing whatever it takes to excel on your exam. **You have come to the right place.** We developed these study materials with one goal in mind: to deliver you the information you need in a format that's concise and easy to use.

In addition to optimizing your guide for the content of the test, we've outlined our recommended steps for breaking down the preparation process into small, attainable goals so you can make sure you stay on track.

We've also analyzed the entire test-taking process, identifying the most common pitfalls and showing how you can overcome them and be ready for any curveball the test throws you.

Standardized testing is one of the biggest obstacles on your road to success, which only increases the importance of doing well in the high-pressure, high-stakes environment of test day. Your results on this test could have a significant impact on your future, and this guide provides the information and practical advice to help you achieve your full potential on test day.

Your success is our success

We would love to hear from you! If you would like to share the story of your exam success or if you have any questions or comments in regard to our products, please contact us at **800-673-8175** or **support@mometrix.com**.

Thanks again for your business and we wish you continued success!

Sincerely,
The Mometrix Test Preparation Team

Need more help? Check out our flashcards at:
http://MometrixFlashcards.com/STS

TABLE OF CONTENTS

Introduction

Thank you for purchasing this resource! You have made the choice to prepare yourself for a test that could have a huge impact on your future, and this guide is designed to help you be fully ready for test day. Obviously, it's important to have a solid understanding of the test material, but you also need to be prepared for the unique environment and stressors of the test, so that you can perform to the best of your abilities.

For this purpose, the first section that appears in this guide is the **Secret Keys**. We've devoted countless hours to meticulously researching what works and what doesn't, and we've boiled down our findings to the five most impactful steps you can take to improve your performance on the test. We start at the beginning with study planning and move through the preparation process, all the way to the testing strategies that will help you get the most out of what you know when you're finally sitting in front of the test.

We recommend that you start preparing for your test as far in advance as possible. However, if you've bought this guide as a last-minute study resource and only have a few days before your test, we recommend that you skip over the first two Secret Keys since they address a long-term study plan.

If you struggle with **test anxiety**, we strongly encourage you to check out our recommendations for how you can overcome it. Test anxiety is a formidable foe, but it can be beaten, and we want to make sure you have the tools you need to defeat it.

1

Secret Key 1: Plan Big, Study Small

There's a lot riding on your performance. If you want to ace this test, you're going to need to keep your skills sharp and the material fresh in your mind. You need a plan that lets you review everything you need to know while still fitting in your schedule. We'll break this strategy down into three categories.

Information Organization

Start with the information you already have: the official test outline. From this, you can make a complete list of all the concepts you need to cover before the test. Organize these concepts into groups that can be studied together, and create a list of any related vocabulary you need to learn so you can brush up on any difficult terms. You'll want to keep this vocabulary list handy once you actually start studying since you may need to add to it along the way.

Time Management

Once you have your set of study concepts, decide how to spread them out over the time you have left before the test. Break your study plan into small, clear goals so you have a manageable task for each day and know exactly what you're doing. Then just focus on one small step at a time. When you manage your time this way, you don't need to spend hours at a time studying. Studying a small block of content for a short period each day helps you retain information better and avoid stressing over how much you have left to do. You can relax knowing that you have a plan to cover everything in time. In order for this strategy to be effective though, you have to start studying early and stick to your schedule. Avoid the exhaustion and futility that comes from last-minute cramming!

Study Environment

The environment you study in has a big impact on your learning. Studying in a coffee shop, while probably more enjoyable, is not likely to be as fruitful as studying in a quiet room. It's important to keep distractions to a minimum. You're only planning to study for a short block of time, so make the most of it. Don't pause to check your phone or get up to find a snack. It's also important to **avoid multitasking**. Research has consistently shown that multitasking will make your studying dramatically less effective. Your study area should also be comfortable and well-lit so you don't have the distraction of straining your eyes or sitting on an uncomfortable chair.

The time of day you study is also important. You want to be rested and alert. Don't wait until just before bedtime. Study when you'll be most likely to comprehend and remember. Even better, if you know what time of day your test will be, set that time aside for study. That way your brain will be used to working on that subject at that specific time and you'll have a better chance of recalling information.

Finally, it can be helpful to team up with others who are studying for the same test. Your actual studying should be done in as isolated an environment as possible, but the work of organizing the information and setting up the study plan can be divided up. In between study sessions, you can discuss with your teammates the concepts that you're all studying and quiz each other on the details. Just be sure that your teammates are as serious about the test as you are. If you find that your study time is being replaced with social time, you might need to find a new team.

Secret Key 2: Make Your Studying Count

You're devoting a lot of time and effort to preparing for this test, so you want to be absolutely certain it will pay off. This means doing more than just reading the content and hoping you can remember it on test day. It's important to make every minute of study count. There are two main areas you can focus on to make your studying count.

Retention

It doesn't matter how much time you study if you can't remember the material. You need to make sure you are retaining the concepts. To check your retention of the information you're learning, try recalling it at later times with minimal prompting. Try carrying around flashcards and glance at one or two from time to time or ask a friend who's also studying for the test to quiz you.

To enhance your retention, look for ways to put the information into practice so that you can apply it rather than simply recalling it. If you're using the information in practical ways, it will be much easier to remember. Similarly, it helps to solidify a concept in your mind if you're not only reading it to yourself but also explaining it to someone else. Ask a friend to let you teach them about a concept you're a little shaky on (or speak aloud to an imaginary audience if necessary). As you try to summarize, define, give examples, and answer your friend's questions, you'll understand the concepts better and they will stay with you longer. Finally, step back for a big picture view and ask yourself how each piece of information fits with the whole subject. When you link the different concepts together and see them working together as a whole, it's easier to remember the individual components.

Finally, practice showing your work on any multi-step problems, even if you're just studying. Writing out each step you take to solve a problem will help solidify the process in your mind, and you'll be more likely to remember it during the test.

Modality

Modality simply refers to the means or method by which you study. Choosing a study modality that fits your own individual learning style is crucial. No two people learn best in exactly the same way, so it's important to know your strengths and use them to your advantage.

4

For example, if you learn best by visualization, focus on visualizing a concept in your mind and draw an image or a diagram. Try color-coding your notes, illustrating them, or creating symbols that will trigger your mind to recall a learned concept. If you learn best by hearing or discussing information, find a study partner who learns the same way or read aloud to yourself. Think about how to put the information in your own words. Imagine that you are giving a lecture on the topic and record yourself so you can listen to it later.

For any learning style, flashcards can be helpful. Organize the information so you can take advantage of spare moments to review. Underline key words or phrases. Use different colors for different categories. Mnemonic devices (such as creating a short list in which every item starts with the same letter) can also help with retention. Find what works best for you and use it to store the information in your mind most effectively and easily.

Secret Key 3: Practice the Right Way

Your success on test day depends not only on how many hours you put into preparing, but also on whether you prepared the right way. It's good to check along the way to see if your studying is paying off. One of the most effective ways to do this is by taking practice tests to evaluate your progress. Practice tests are useful because they show exactly where you need to improve. Every time you take a practice test, pay special attention to these three groups of questions:

- The questions you got wrong
- The questions you had to guess on, even if you guessed right
- The questions you found difficult or slow to work through

This will show you exactly what your weak areas are, and where you need to devote more study time. Ask yourself why each of these questions gave you trouble. Was it because you didn't understand the material? Was it because you didn't remember the vocabulary? Do you need more repetitions on this type of question to build speed and confidence? Dig into those questions and figure out how you can strengthen your weak areas as you go back to review the material.

 Additionally, many practice tests have a section explaining the answer choices. It can be tempting to read the explanation and think that you now have a good understanding of the concept. However, an explanation likely only covers part of the question's broader context. Even if the explanation makes perfect sense, **go back and investigate** every concept related to the question until you're positive you have a thorough understanding.

As you go along, keep in mind that the practice test is just that: practice. Memorizing these questions and answers will not be very helpful on the actual test because it is unlikely to have any of the same exact questions. If you only know the right answers to the sample questions, you won't be prepared for the real thing. **Study the concepts** until you understand them fully, and then you'll be able to answer any question that shows up on the test.

It's important to wait on the practice tests until you're ready. If you take a test on your first day of study, you may be overwhelmed by the amount of material covered and how much you need to learn. Work up to it gradually.

On test day, you'll need to be prepared for answering questions, managing your time, and using the test-taking strategies you've learned. It's a lot to balance, like a mental marathon that will have a big impact on your future. Like training for a marathon, you'll need to start slowly and work your way up. When test day arrives, you'll be ready.

Start with the strategies you've read in the first two Secret Keys—plan your course and study in the way that works best for you. If you have time, consider using multiple study resources to get different approaches to the same concepts. It can be helpful to see difficult concepts from more than one angle. Then find a good source for practice tests. Many times, the test website will suggest potential study resources or provide sample tests.

Practice Test Strategy

If you're able to find at least three practice tests, we recommend this strategy:

UNTIMED AND OPEN-BOOK PRACTICE

Take the first test with no time constraints and with your notes and study guide handy. Take your time and focus on applying the strategies you've learned.

TIMED AND OPEN-BOOK PRACTICE

Take the second practice test open-book as well, but set a timer and practice pacing yourself to finish in time.

TIMED AND CLOSED-BOOK PRACTICE

Take any other practice tests as if it were test day. Set a timer and put away your study materials. Sit at a table or desk in a quiet room, imagine yourself at the testing center, and answer questions as quickly and accurately as possible.

Keep repeating timed and closed-book tests on a regular basis until you run out of practice tests or it's time for the actual test. Your mind will be ready for the schedule and stress of test day, and you'll be able to focus on recalling the material you've learned.

Secret Key 4: Pace Yourself

Once you're fully prepared for the material on the test, your biggest challenge on test day will be managing your time. Just knowing that the clock is ticking can make you panic even if you have plenty of time left. Work on pacing yourself so you can build confidence against the time constraints of the exam. Pacing is a difficult skill to master, especially in a high-pressure environment, so **practice is vital**.

Set time expectations for your pace based on how much time is available. For example, if a section has 60 questions and the time limit is 30 minutes, you know you have to average 30 seconds or less per question in order to answer them all. Although 30 seconds is the hard limit, set 25 seconds per question as your goal, so you reserve extra time to spend on harder questions. When you budget extra time for the harder questions, you no longer have any reason to stress when those questions take longer to answer.

Don't let this time expectation distract you from working through the test at a calm, steady pace, but keep it in mind so you don't spend too much time on any one question. Recognize that taking extra time on one question you don't understand may keep you from answering two that you do understand later in the test. If your time limit for a question is up and you're still not sure of the answer, mark it and move on, and come back to it later if the time and the test format allow. If the testing format doesn't allow you to return to earlier questions, just make an educated guess; then put it out of your mind and move on.

On the easier questions, be careful not to rush. It may seem wise to hurry through them so you have more time for the challenging ones, but it's not worth missing one if you know the concept and just didn't take the time to read the question fully. Work efficiently but make sure you understand the question and have looked at all of the answer choices, since more than one may seem right at first.

Even if you're paying attention to the time, you may find yourself a little behind at some point. You should speed up to get back on track, but do so wisely. Don't panic; just take a few seconds less on each question until you're caught up. Don't guess without thinking, but do look through the answer choices and eliminate any you know are wrong. If you can get down to two choices, it is often worthwhile to guess from those. Once you've chosen an answer, move on and don't dwell on any that you skipped or had to hurry through. If a question was taking too long, chances are it was one of the harder ones, so you weren't as likely to get it right anyway.

On the other hand, if you find yourself getting ahead of schedule, it may be beneficial to slow down a little. The more quickly you work, the more likely you are to make a careless mistake that will affect your score. You've budgeted time for each question, so don't be afraid to spend that time. Practice an efficient but careful pace to get the most out of the time you have.

Secret Key 5: Have a Plan for Guessing

When you're taking the test, you may find yourself stuck on a question. Some of the answer choices seem better than others, but you don't see the one answer choice that is obviously correct. What do you do?

The scenario described above is very common, yet most test takers have not effectively prepared for it. Developing and practicing a plan for guessing may be one of the single most effective uses of your time as you get ready for the exam.

In developing your plan for guessing, there are three questions to address:

- When should you start the guessing process?
- How should you narrow down the choices?
- Which answer should you choose?

When to Start the Guessing Process

Unless your plan for guessing is to select C every time (which, despite its merits, is not what we recommend), you need to leave yourself enough time to apply your answer elimination strategies. Since you have a limited amount of time for each question, that means that if you're going to give yourself the best shot at guessing correctly, you have to decide quickly whether or not you will guess.

Of course, the best-case scenario is that you don't have to guess at all, so first, see if you can answer the question based on your knowledge of the subject and basic reasoning skills. Focus on the key words in the question and try to jog your memory of related topics. Give yourself a chance to bring the knowledge to mind, but once you realize that you don't have (or you can't access) the knowledge you need to answer the question, it's time to start the guessing process.

It's almost always better to start the guessing process too early than too late. It only takes a few seconds to remember something and answer the question from knowledge. Carefully eliminating wrong answer choices takes longer. Plus, going through the process of eliminating answer choices can actually help jog your memory.

Summary: Start the guessing process as soon as you decide that you can't answer the question based on your knowledge.

How to Narrow Down the Choices

The next chapter in this book (**Test-Taking Strategies**) includes a wide range of strategies for how to approach questions and how to look for answer choices to eliminate. You will definitely want to read those carefully, practice them, and figure out which ones work best for you. Here though, we're going to address a mindset rather than a particular strategy.

Your odds of guessing an answer correctly depend on how many options you are choosing from.

Number of options left	5	4	3	2	1
Odds of guessing correctly	20%	25%	33%	50%	100%

You can see from this chart just how valuable it is to be able to eliminate incorrect answers and make an educated guess, but there are two things that many test takers do that cause them to miss out on the benefits of guessing:

- Accidentally eliminating the correct answer
- Selecting an answer based on an impression

We'll look at the first one here, and the second one in the next section.

To avoid accidentally eliminating the correct answer, we recommend a thought exercise called **the $5 challenge**. In this challenge, you only eliminate an answer choice from contention if you are willing to bet $5 on it being wrong. Why $5? Five dollars is a small but not insignificant amount of money. It's an amount you could

afford to lose but wouldn't want to throw away. And while losing $5 once might not hurt too much, doing it twenty times will set you back $100. In the same way, each small decision you make—eliminating a choice here, guessing on a question there—won't by itself impact your score very much, but when you put them all together, they can make a big difference. By holding each answer choice elimination decision to a higher standard, you can reduce the risk of accidentally eliminating the correct answer.

The $5 challenge can also be applied in a positive sense: If you are willing to bet $5 that an answer choice *is* correct, go ahead and mark it as correct.

Summary: Only eliminate an answer choice if you are willing to bet $5 that it is wrong.

Which Answer to Choose

You're taking the test. You've run into a hard question and decided you'll have to guess. You've eliminated all the answer choices you're willing to bet $5 on. Now you have to pick an answer. Why do we even need to talk about this? Why can't you just pick whichever one you feel like when the time comes?

The answer to these questions is that if you don't come into the test with a plan, you'll rely on your impression to select an answer choice, and if you do that, you risk falling into a trap. The test writers know that everyone who takes their test will be guessing on some of the questions, so they intentionally write wrong answer choices to seem plausible. You still have to pick an answer though, and if the wrong answer choices are designed to look right, how can you ever be sure that you're not falling for their trap? The best solution we've found to this dilemma is to take the decision out of your hands entirely. Here is the process we recommend:

Once you've eliminated any choices that you are confident (willing to bet $5) are wrong, select the first remaining choice as your answer.

Whether you choose to select the first remaining choice, the second, or the last, the important thing is that you use some preselected standard. Using this approach guarantees that you will not be enticed into selecting an answer choice that looks right, because you are not basing your decision on how the answer choices look.

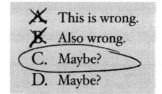

This is not meant to make you question your knowledge. Instead, it is to help you recognize the difference between your knowledge and your impressions. There's a huge difference between thinking an answer is right because of what you know, and thinking an answer is right because it looks or sounds like it should be right.

Summary: To ensure that your selection is appropriately random, make a predetermined selection from among all answer choices you have not eliminated.

Test-Taking Strategies

This section contains a list of test-taking strategies that you may find helpful as you work through the test. By taking what you know and applying logical thought, you can maximize your chances of answering any question correctly!

It is very important to realize that every question is different and every person is different: no single strategy will work on every question, and no single strategy will work for every person. That's why we've included all of them here, so you can try them out and determine which ones work best for different types of questions and which ones work best for you.

Question Strategies

⊘ READ CAREFULLY

Read the question and the answer choices carefully. Don't miss the question because you misread the terms. You have plenty of time to read each question thoroughly and make sure you understand what is being asked. Yet a happy medium must be attained, so don't waste too much time. You must read carefully and efficiently.

⊘ CONTEXTUAL CLUES

Look for contextual clues. If the question includes a word you are not familiar with, look at the immediate context for some indication of what the word might mean. Contextual clues can often give you all the information you need to decipher the meaning of an unfamiliar word. Even if you can't determine the meaning, you may be able to narrow down the possibilities enough to make a solid guess at the answer to the question.

⊘ PREFIXES

If you're having trouble with a word in the question or answer choices, try dissecting it. Take advantage of every clue that the word might include. Prefixes can be a huge help. Usually, they allow you to determine a basic meaning. *Pre-* means before, *post-* means after, *pro-* is positive, *de-* is negative. From prefixes, you can get an idea of the general meaning of the word and try to put it into context.

⊘ HEDGE WORDS

Watch out for critical hedge words, such as *likely, may, can, sometimes, often, almost, mostly, usually, generally, rarely*, and *sometimes*. Question writers insert these hedge phrases to cover every possibility. Often an answer choice will be wrong simply because it leaves no room for exception. Be on guard for answer choices that have definitive words such as *exactly* and *always*.

⊘ Switchback Words

Stay alert for *switchbacks*. These are the words and phrases frequently used to alert you to shifts in thought. The most common switchback words are *but*, *although*, and *however*. Others include *nevertheless*, *on the other hand*, *even though*, *while*, *in spite of*, *despite*, and *regardless of*. Switchback words are important to catch because they can change the direction of the question or an answer choice.

⊘ Face Value

When in doubt, use common sense. Accept the situation in the problem at face value. Don't read too much into it. These problems will not require you to make wild assumptions. If you have to go beyond creativity and warp time or space in order to have an answer choice fit the question, then you should move on and consider the other answer choices. These are normal problems rooted in reality. The applicable relationship or explanation may not be readily apparent, but it is there for you to figure out. Use your common sense to interpret anything that isn't clear.

Answer Choice Strategies

⊘ Answer Selection

The most thorough way to pick an answer choice is to identify and eliminate wrong answers until only one is left, then confirm it is the correct answer. Sometimes an answer choice may immediately seem right, but be careful. The test writers will usually put more than one reasonable answer choice on each question, so take a second to read all of them and make sure that the other choices are not equally obvious. As long as you have time left, it is better to read every answer choice than to pick the first one that looks right without checking the others.

⊘ Answer Choice Families

An answer choice family consists of two (in rare cases, three) answer choices that are very similar in construction and cannot all be true at the same time. If you see two answer choices that are direct opposites or parallels, one of them is usually the correct answer. For instance, if one answer choice says that quantity x increases and another either says that quantity x decreases (opposite) or says that quantity y increases (parallel), then those answer choices would fall into the same family. An answer choice that doesn't match the construction of the answer choice family is more likely to be incorrect. Most questions will not have answer choice families, but when they do appear, you should be prepared to recognize them.

⊘ Eliminate Answers

Eliminate answer choices as soon as you realize they are wrong, but make sure you consider all possibilities. If you are eliminating answer choices and realize that the last one you are left with is also wrong, don't panic. Start over and consider each choice again. There may be something you missed the first time that you will realize on the second pass.

14

⊘ Avoid Fact Traps

Don't be distracted by an answer choice that is factually true but doesn't answer the question. You are looking for the choice that answers the question. Stay focused on what the question is asking for so you don't accidentally pick an answer that is true but incorrect. Always go back to the question and make sure the answer choice you've selected actually answers the question and is not merely a true statement.

⊘ Extreme Statements

In general, you should avoid answers that put forth extreme actions as standard practice or proclaim controversial ideas as established fact. An answer choice that states the "process should be used in certain situations, if…" is much more likely to be correct than one that states the "process should be discontinued completely." The first is a calm rational statement and doesn't even make a definitive, uncompromising stance, using a hedge word *if* to provide wiggle room, whereas the second choice is far more extreme.

⊘ Benchmark

As you read through the answer choices and you come across one that seems to answer the question well, mentally select that answer choice. This is not your final answer, but it's the one that will help you evaluate the other answer choices. The one that you selected is your benchmark or standard for judging each of the other answer choices. Every other answer choice must be compared to your benchmark. That choice is correct until proven otherwise by another answer choice beating it. If you find a better answer, then that one becomes your new benchmark. Once you've decided that no other choice answers the question as well as your benchmark, you have your final answer.

⊘ Predict the Answer

Before you even start looking at the answer choices, it is often best to try to predict the answer. When you come up with the answer on your own, it is easier to avoid distractions and traps because you will know exactly what to look for. The right answer choice is unlikely to be word-for-word what you came up with, but it should be a close match. Even if you are confident that you have the right answer, you should still take the time to read each option before moving on.

General Strategies

⊘ Tough Questions

If you are stumped on a problem or it appears too hard or too difficult, don't waste time. Move on! Remember though, if you can quickly check for obviously incorrect answer choices, your chances of guessing correctly are greatly improved. Before you completely give up, at least try to knock out a couple of possible answers. Eliminate what you can and then guess at the remaining answer choices before moving on.

⊘ CHECK YOUR WORK

Since you will probably not know every term listed and the answer to every question, it is important that you get credit for the ones that you do know. Don't miss any questions through careless mistakes. If at all possible, try to take a second to look back over your answer selection and make sure you've selected the correct answer choice and haven't made a costly careless mistake (such as marking an answer choice that you didn't mean to mark). This quick double check should more than pay for itself in caught mistakes for the time it costs.

⊘ PACE YOURSELF

It's easy to be overwhelmed when you're looking at a page full of questions; your mind is confused and full of random thoughts, and the clock is ticking down faster than you would like. Calm down and maintain the pace that you have set for yourself. Especially as you get down to the last few minutes of the test, don't let the small numbers on the clock make you panic. As long as you are on track by monitoring your pace, you are guaranteed to have time for each question.

⊘ DON'T RUSH

It is very easy to make errors when you are in a hurry. Maintaining a fast pace in answering questions is pointless if it makes you miss questions that you would have gotten right otherwise. Test writers like to include distracting information and wrong answers that seem right. Taking a little extra time to avoid careless mistakes can make all the difference in your test score. Find a pace that allows you to be confident in the answers that you select.

⊘ KEEP MOVING

Panicking will not help you pass the test, so do your best to stay calm and keep moving. Taking deep breaths and going through the answer elimination steps you practiced can help to break through a stress barrier and keep your pace.

Final Notes

The combination of a solid foundation of content knowledge and the confidence that comes from practicing your plan for applying that knowledge is the key to maximizing your performance on test day. As your foundation of content knowledge is built up and strengthened, you'll find that the strategies included in this chapter become more and more effective in helping you quickly sift through the distractions and traps of the test to isolate the correct answer.

Now that you're preparing to move forward into the test content chapters of this book, be sure to keep your goal in mind. As you read, think about how you will be able to apply this information on the test. If you've already seen sample questions for the test and you have an idea of the question format and style, try to come up with questions of your own that you can answer based on what you're reading. This will give you valuable practice applying your knowledge in the same ways you can expect to on test day.

Good luck and good studying!

Safety Program Implementation and Management

Job Safety/Hazard Analysis

HAZARD

The Occupational Safety and Health Administration (OSHA) defines a **hazard** as any condition that, if left uncontrolled, could result in an injury.

Hazards can be classified as physical, environmental, chemical, or biological. **Physical hazards** include anything that can impact the body, such as falls, electricity, or high pressure. **Environmental hazards** include heat, cold, and noise. **Chemical hazards** are any harm that can be caused by exposure to a chemical, such as chemical burns and toxins. **Biological hazards** take the form of molds, bloodborne pathogens, animals, or insects.

JOB HAZARD ANALYSIS

A **job hazard analysis (JHA)** is a formalized process of identifying hazards and unsafe practices related to a specific job. Such an analysis can be applied to a single job or to a single task associated with a job. For example, a JHA may be conducted for a warehouse employee or for stacking bagged materials.

The primary goal is to identify opportunities to **modify** the job to avoid unsafe conditions and practices that could result in an occupational injury. The job is broken down into tasks and then into steps. Each step is evaluated for potential hazards. Once the **hazards** are identified, the **risk** can be determined, and then **controls** can be implemented to reduce the chances of an injury.

STEPS OF A JOB HAZARD ANALYSIS

A formalized **job hazard analysis (JHA)** is used to identify and proactively address potential risks of injury associated with a job or a task. First, the job or task to be analyzed must be **identified** in the workplace. Next, the job is divided into **sequential steps** referred to as "tasks." For example, the job of "moving pallets with a forklift" could be broken down into the tasks of "driving to location, picking up load, transferring load, depositing load." Then, each step is **evaluated** for potential hazards as well as conditions that could potentially result in an incident. In the warehouse example, the hazards associated with "transferring load" could include unbalanced loading, dropping the load, striking pedestrians, tipping, etc.

The final step in a hazard analysis is to **develop solutions** for all identified hazards. The hazards must be removed or reduced to make the job safer and decrease the risk of injury. Hazard controls may be prioritized and implemented based on cost or effectiveness. For the risk of striking a pedestrian, the control could include "using horn whenever approaching a corner."

19

JOB PRIORITIZATION

Although any job or task could benefit from a **job hazard analysis (JHA)**, a safety professional should prioritize JHAs based on injury frequency, rate, and severity as well as for new tasks.

An indicator that an assessment should be made for a job would be a high **frequency** of injuries. Any job or task that continues to result in injuries, even if they are seemingly minor injuries, should be a candidate for a JHA before a major injury occurs.

Those jobs that have a high **rate** of injury, expressed as number of injuries per worker doing the job, should also be considered for a JHA. A high injury rate indicates that the risk is not based on the individuals performing the job but may be related to how the job is being performed.

If a job or task could result in a serious injury, referred to as the task's **severity**, then a JHA may be appropriate. Even though every injury should be taken seriously, a job that could cause injuries resulting in hospitalizations, lost days of work, or even fatalities should be given extra attention as to how it could be made safer to avoid those negative outcomes.

Finally, **new** jobs or tasks that are unfamiliar to workers have a high opportunity for mistakes that can lead to injuries. New ways of working, new motions, new processes, and new equipment have inherent risks that need to be identified and controlled to avoid the occurrence of injuries.

SOLUTIONS MAKING TASKS LESS HAZARDOUS

The final step in a job hazard analysis is to develop **solutions** to control the risk of injury. For each hazard, a control should be identified that improves the safety of the task and does not introduce any additional hazards. Solutions may include reworking the task, selecting different equipment, changing the procedure, or reducing the frequency of the task.

Finding a **new way** to do the task could be as simple as outsourcing hazardous work or automating a previously manual job. Purchasing adjustable workstations is an example of selecting **different equipment** to avoid ergonomic injuries for staff at their workstations. Reducing the amount of time an employee works in a noisy section of the factory is a **procedural change** to reduce the impact of occupational noise. Finally, rotating a worker from an assembly line to housekeeping will **lessen the amount** of repetitive motion they experience in a day, which can reduce the risk of soft tissue injuries.

UPDATING A JOB HAZARD ANALYSIS

A **job hazard analysis (JHA)** evaluates a series of tasks and the associated hazard. The goal is to identify potential controls prior to doing the work, so the risks of injury are reduced. A JHA should be updated:

- When an **injury** has occurred in performing the job, indicating that the hazards are not properly controlled.
- When the process has been **changed**, including the introduction of new or different equipment. Any change to a process should be evaluated for its impact on injury risk from either changing the risk or introducing new risks.
- At specified **time intervals** to ensure the JHA remains relevant and current. This also allows the safety professional to be aware of any changes in the workplace that may not have been communicated.

The Globally Harmonized System (GHS)

GLOBALLY HARMONIZED SYSTEM

The **Globally Harmonized System (GHS)** of Classification and Labeling of Chemicals is an international system used to convey the hazardous properties of materials of trade to those who **handle** or **use** them. Developed by the United Nations, the GHS outlines how materials should be **labeled** to unambiguously convey potential hazards to employees, transporters, and handlers.

The GHS uses nine (9) **hazard classes** to describe the risks associated with any material, keeping in mind that a material may be assigned to more than one class. The system describes the label requirements, such as the use of signal words, pictograms, hazard statements, and precautionary statements.

CHEMICAL HAZARD CLASSES

The **Globally Harmonized System** of Classification and Labeling of Chemicals **(GHS)** uses a system of nine (9) **hazard classes** to identify the hazards associated with a material. A chemical may belong to more than one class, based on its properties. Those classes are:

- **Corrosive**—the ability to destroy metal and flesh
- **Toxic**—the ability to cause illness or death
- **Health hazard**—the ability to cause injury to organs or organ systems
- **Irritant** or **sensitizer**—irritants cause itching or burning to the eyes or skin, while sensitizers make an individual more susceptible to a chemical during future exposures, which can appear as an allergic rash
- **Environment**—these chemicals can cause short- or long-term damage to ecosystems
- **Flammables**—used for flammable and combustible chemicals which can cause or initiate fires
- **Explosives**—materials that react violently to produce high pressure which can damage containers and nearby objects, including people

- **Oxidizers**—materials that increase or accelerate burning rates due to the presence of oxygen in their makeup
- **Compressed gases**—gases stored under pressure that present a high-pressure hazard as well as the hazard of the material they contain

HAZARD COMMUNICATION PROGRAM

A **Hazard Communication Program**, as required by 29 CFR 1910.1200, describes the way in which an employer will **inform** employees of the hazards associated with the chemicals they may use or encounter while performing their jobs.

The standard, based on the Globally Harmonized System of Classification and Labeling of Chemicals (GHS), requires employers to convey the hazards, safety measures, and other important information clearly, so employees can handle chemicals safely. The employer must have a **written** hazard communication ("HazCom") program that addresses

- proper **labeling** of containers or other **forms of warning**,
- how **safety data sheets (SDS)** will be managed and made available to employees, and
- the required topics for employee **training**.

SAFETY DATA SHEETS

The Hazard Communication Standard requires that an employer maintain **safety data sheets (SDS)** for any hazardous chemical that an employee may use or handle while performing their job. An SDS is an informational document prepared by the **manufacturer or distributor** of the chemical and is used to convey hazard information to the end user or handler of the product. The SDS is divided into sixteen (16) sections, each having different information.

The SDS contains the **name** of the chemical and the ingredients if it is a mixture. The sheet also has the name and **contact information** of the manufacturer as well as the **hazards** the material presents to employees. The sheets also have safe **handling** and **storage** requirements as well as what **protective equipment** is recommended while using the material. **Health effects** and **exposure limits** are presented, so an employee can determine what the safe levels are and what symptoms they could experience if they are exposed to the substance. Other information regarding **medical treatment** and **firefighting** measures is also provided on the document, in addition to chemical and physical **properties** of the substance.

TRAINING REQUIREMENTS

The Hazard Communication Program, under 29 CFR 1910.1200, is based on the Globally Harmonized System of Classification and Labeling of Chemicals (GHS). It describes the method by which employees must be **informed** of the dangers of the chemicals they encounter in the workplace. The standard identifies two occasions when employee training is required—upon their **initial assignment** and whenever a **new substance** is introduced into the workplace. If many different substances are present in the workplace, the employer can opt to train employees on the **general**

22

classes of hazards and how to recognize their presence instead of each individual substance.

The standard does not explicitly require recurring refresher training for employees. However, employers should evaluate the effectiveness of their training program and determine if initial training is adequate for employees to understand and safely apply the standard.

Equipment Inspections

EQUIPMENT INSPECTIONS

An inspection is a **visual assessment** of the condition of a piece of equipment. Equipment should be inspected **before** every use to ensure it is in a proper and safe condition for use. For powered tools and equipment, the power supply should be intact and functional, such as cords that are undamaged and fuel tanks that are not leaking. Guards and protective devices should be present, in good condition, and functional. The equipment should not be visibly broken, worn, or missing parts or pieces, and it should be in good condition.

SAFETY EQUIPMENT INSPECTIONS

Similar to mechanical equipment, safety equipment should always be **inspected** before work begins. Whether it is a machine guard, indicator light, or respirator, the **functionality** and ability to protect workers should always be evaluated prior to operation. Safety equipment that is damaged, missing parts, or not functioning correctly will not provide any risk reduction. Chemical-resistant gloves that have holes will not prevent a corrosive from getting on a worker's hands. A respirator missing a valve will not keep asbestos fibers out of an employee's lungs. A fractured protective shield can shatter if struck by a projectile. Safety equipment can only be effective if it is in good working order.

EVALUATING ALL ITEMS OF AN EQUIPMENT INSPECTION

Equipment inspections are used to verify that an item is in good working order and is safe to use. In order to standardize the inspection process, a **checklist** should be developed. The checklist serves two purposes—it ensures that all necessary items are checked prior to use and serves as a **written record** of the inspection. The checklist should indicate the required **frequency** of the inspection, such as prior to each use, weekly, or monthly, as recommended by the manufacturer or required by standard. In addition to the items inspected, the checklist should record who conducted the inspection and when.

RESPONSIBLE PARTY FOR EQUIPMENT INSPECTIONS

Under the **General Duty Clause**, employers are required to minimize hazards at work. To that end, the **employer** is responsible for implementing an inspection program to evaluate the workplace for hazards and make sure that equipment is in good condition and safety measures are in place, adequate, and appropriate. Additionally, **employees** should conduct their own inspections to verify the condition of equipment prior to use. In some cases, such as for protective equipment, the employee is required to conduct checks to evaluate the condition and integrity of the equipment before donning it.

Safety Training

EMPLOYEE TRAINING

The employer must provide training to all employees regarding the **recognition and avoidance of hazards** at the workplace. Additionally, the employer must instruct the employees on how to **control or eliminate** health and safety hazards or other conditions that could expose the employee to injury or illness.

OSHA places a high value on **effective** training. Thus, OSHA standards require training whenever an employee will conduct tasks with specific or elevated hazards, such as responding to hazardous substance spills, electrical work, or working at heights. Training content must be **understandable** to the employees, meaning that it may need to be conducted in languages other than English.

TRAINING PROGRAM

OSHA requires that safety training be **effective**, meaning that behavioral modification or learning has occurred. OSHA has explained that simply having employees review written programs is not considered an effective means of information exchange. An effective training program is one that:

- establishes clear and achievable **objectives**,
- leverages the many aspects of **adult learning** (visual learners, audio learners, and kinetic learners),
- is **understandable** by all attendees in terms of level of complexity and primary language, and
- has an **evaluation** to determine whether learning has occurred, by way of written examination or practical demonstration of the new skill.

SAFETY TRAINING PROGRAM FREQUENCY

The employer is required to inform employees of hazards in the workplace, as well as protective measures available to reduce the risk associated with those hazards. OSHA puts a high degree of value on "**effective training**," meaning that the employer must verify that the employee **understands** the information and can follow the safety programs. For standards that require training, the **OSHA standard** will have a section that outlines when and how often the training should occur. For example, bloodborne pathogen training is required annually, whereas hazard communication training is required before an employee uses hazardous substances.

LOCATION OF CONTENT

OSHA emphasizes employee **training** as an effective method for conveying information to employees. OSHA has accepted in-person as well as computer-based training as acceptable methods for training. The **content** of a training program is dependent on the topic and can be found in the **OSHA standards** within 29 CFR 1910. Standards that require training will list the **minimum topics** that must be covered by an employer to satisfy the training component as well as require training **records** to be retained in employee files. A common inquiry during an on-site OSHA inspection is proof that employee training on the issue associated with the inspection has occurred and at the required frequency, as stated in the relevant standard.

Confined Space

CONFINED SPACE

A **confined space** is any space that a worker can enter but has limited access and is not intended for human occupancy. In order to be considered a confined space, the area must meet all of the following criteria:

- The space has **limited access**, meaning that the way to enter the space is a non-standard entry point, such as a hatch, manhole, or other non-door entrance. These limited access points can **impede** or prohibit a quick exit in the event of an emergency. A space may have more than one entrance and still be considered a confined space.
- The space is large enough for a person to **enter** and do work. In this case, a worker can get their entire body into the space and could become trapped inside.
- Finally, the space is not intended for **human occupancy**, meaning it is not a room, office, or other designated space. Examples of confined spaces include excavations, crawl spaces, pipes, service pits, and underground utility vaults.

PERMIT-REQUIRED CONFINED SPACES

A **permit-required confined** space meets all the criteria of a confined space but also has the potential of a **hazardous atmosphere**, has material that can engulf and **trap** a worker, has **sloping walls** or a **tapered floor** that can trap a worker, or contains any other **recognized hazard**. Essentially, they are extremely hazardous confined spaces. Utility vaults with decomposing plant material can have toxic atmospheres, pits where flammable chemicals have spilled can become flammable or oxygen deficient, and a subfloor may narrow to a point where turning around is difficult. Any of those conditions can turn a confined space into a permit-required confined space.

It must be remembered that not every confined space requires a permit to enter. However, if the space has the potential for any one of the other hazardous conditions, it is required to have a permit issued prior to entry.

ENTRY PERMIT

When a confined space presents additional hazards that can impede escape or presents a significant hazard to entrants, additional safety measures must be taken. Significant hazards include hazardous atmospheres, materials that can trap or engulf the entrant, sloping or tapering floors, or other recognized hazards. A **written document** that describes the hazards on controls, called a **permit**, must be completed prior to entry and posted at the entry point. The permit must list the following:

- The space that is to be entered
- The work to be performed in the space
- The date and duration of the work
- The name or other unique identifier of all entrants
- How a hazardous atmospheric condition will be detected
- Name(s) of attendant(s)
- Supervisor responsible for the work and the space
- Hazards known to be present in the space
- How the hazards have been controlled
- Acceptable entry conditions
- Results of any air monitoring
- Method of communicating with entrants
- Required protective equipment, testing equipment, communication equipment, and rescue equipment being used
- Any other permits being issued for the space

CONDITIONS TRIGGERING NEED FOR A PERMIT

Each year, **confined spaces** are responsible for numerous deaths. Confined spaces, such as utility vaults and crawl spaces, pose specific hazards to workers due to their configuration, limited air flow, or being below grade. These include hazardous atmospheres, the possibility of entrapment or engulfment, the cross-sectional configuration of the space, and other recognized hazards within the space.

The configuration and location of a confined space can result in a potentially **hazardous atmosphere**, which would then require a permit to enter safely. Toxic gases or flammable vapors can settle or become trapped in these spaces, increasing the risk to entrants. Gases or vapors can push oxygen out of these spaces, making the atmosphere oxygen deficient and creating a potential for suffocation.

Tanks that hold solid materials which can **trap or engulf** an employee, making escape difficult or impossible. **Sloping floors or converging sides** where the cross-sectional area decreases can make it difficult for an employee to escape in an emergency. Lastly, any other **recognized hazard** in the space, such as electrical lines or water sources, will have an increased risk to the entrant, where a permit to enter can increase the safety of the work to be conducted in that area.

REQUIRED PERSONNEL

Due to the increased hazards associated with a permit-required confined space, 29 CFR 1910.146 identifies three specific **personnel required** to be present to reduce the risks of working in these spaces: authorized entrants, attendants, and entry supervisors.

An **authorized entrant** is any worker who will be physically entering the space. This person must be authorized by the entry supervisor and have undergone specific training on the hazards presented by the space. The entrant must know how to use all equipment available to mitigate the anticipated and known hazards, including recovery equipment. The entrant must understand the alarm system that would require an immediate evacuation and be able to recognize conditions that would require an evacuation.

An **attendant** is an employee who is always stationed outside of the space. They must understand the hazards within the space and how changing conditions may impact entrants. The attendant must account for all entrants in the event of an emergency condition by tracking who enters and exits. The attendant maintains communication with the entrants. The entrant keeps non-approved personnel from entering the space and is responsible for summoning rescue personnel in the event of an emergency.

The **entry supervisor** must be trained in the hazards present in the space and indications of employee exposure. The supervisor is responsible for checking and verifying the **entry permit** as well as verifying that the atmosphere is appropriate for the work to be performed. They are also responsible for ensuring that **rescue services** are available and that any **communication** device for summoning them is functioning properly. Finally, the entry supervisor approves all employees who are allowed to enter the space.

VENTILATION

Due to their location and internal configuration, confined spaces typically lack **air circulation**. Without proper air exchanges, these spaces have the potential for gases or vapors to accumulate, which can lead to a **hazardous atmosphere** that would require a permit to enter. A hazardous atmosphere can be one that is oxygen deficient (less than 19.5% oxygen), oxygen rich (greater than 23.5% oxygen), flammable (exceeding 10% of the lower flammable limit), or toxic (exceeding published exposure limits).

Ventilation, which is the introduction or removal of air from a space, can lower the levels of flammable or toxic chemicals by circulating in fresh air. Ventilation can also be used to **stabilize** the oxygen level. Ventilation should support all entries into confined spaces with atmospheric hazards. Fans should ventilate the space prior to entry and continue to run while workers are in the space. This will work to continually push fresh air into the space. Ventilation systems must be installed to prevent short-circuiting, where the contaminated exhaust air is pulled back into the space by the blower. Air monitoring should be used to assess the effectiveness of the ventilation system in maintaining safe atmospheric levels.

NON-ENTRY RECOVERY SYSTEMS

Due to the increased hazards in permit-required confined spaces, the employer must provide a means for **non-entry recovery** of any authorized entrant that may become debilitated and unable to escape on their own. A system must be in place before entry unless that system will itself pose a hazard or not successfully recover the entrant. In those instances, the employer must have a trained, staffed, and equipped rescue team on standby during the entry.

Any non-entry retrieval system, typically a **pulley system** mounted to a tripod or other support system, must be attached to each authorized entrant by way of a chest or body **harness**, with the **retrieval line** attachment in the center of the back. Only in cases where a back-mounted retrieval line is impractical can a wrist or ankle line be used. The retrieval line must be attached to a **mechanical device**, so the rescue can begin as soon as necessary. Any vertical confined space that is more than five (5) feet deep requires a mechanical retrieval device, mounted to a tripod stationed over the entrance to the space.

Personal Protective Equipment (PPE)

PERSONAL PROTECTIVE EQUIPMENT

Personal protective equipment (PPE) is any device worn by an individual that is designed to protect them from a **physical** or **chemical** hazard. PPE is typically divided into **categories** based on the body part it is designed to protect—head, face/eyes, respiratory, body, hands, and feet.

PPE includes hard hats, safety glasses or face shields, earplugs or earmuffs, filtering facepieces and respirators, fall harnesses, chemical protective clothing, cut protective gloves, and safety shoes. Specialized clothing, such as cold or warm weather gear, protective sleeves, high-visibility garments, and kneepads that are designed to control a physical hazard are also considered PPE.

LIMITATIONS

Personal protective equipment (PPE) is generally considered the **last line** of defense for protecting workers, after engineering controls and administrative controls. PPE neither removes the hazard nor reduces the individual's exposure. The hazard is still present, and the employee is still near or in contact with the hazard. PPE simply provides a barrier to the hazard and is dependent on proper **selection, care, wearing,** and **maintenance** to protect a worker. If that barrier is modified, broken, worn incorrectly, or otherwise **compromised**, the employee is **exposed** to the hazard.

In an example where a cylinder containing a toxic gas is leaking, an employee must enter the room to tighten the connection. If the safety professional elects to rely solely on PPE, this would involve allowing an employee to enter the room while wearing a respirator. By choosing PPE instead of ventilating the room, the control would not remove the gas nor reduce its concentration below dangerous levels. Thus, if the respirator fails, is not worn properly, is damaged, or becomes overloaded, the employee is exposed.

RESPONSIBLE PARTY FOR DETERMINING PPE

The **employer** is required to assess the workplace to determine which hazards are present. A part of this job hazard assessment (JHA), per 29 CFR 1910.132, is to determine whether personal protective equipment (PPE) would be suitable for protecting employees from the identified hazards. Therefore, the employer is required to **select** and **make available** properly sized equipment that is **appropriate** for the hazards, communicate the hazards that are known and their levels, and describe when the equipment must be worn and why the equipment was selected.

TRAINING TOPICS

If an employer determines that personal protective equipment (PPE) can be used to control hazards at the workplace, the employer is required under 29 CFR 1910.132 to train employees. The training for PPE must include:

- The circumstances or **conditions** when PPE must be worn
- The required PPE **components** (such as hard hat, gloves, respirator, or work boots)
- How to properly put on (**"don"**), take off (**"doff"**), and **wear** the required PPE
- The **limitations** of the PPE
- The proper care, maintenance, useful life, and proper disposal of all PPE

EYE PROTECTION

The eyes are very sensitive to chemicals and particulates, such as dirt and debris. Chemicals that enter the eye can cause temporary or permanent damage. Metal or wood slivers can penetrate the eye, resulting in serious injury. Thus, proper eye protection, in the form of safety glasses, safety goggles, or face shields, is selected based on the risk presented to the eyes or face.

Safety glasses protect the eyes from **flying solid debris**, such as dust, dirt, and metal shavings. If the eyes must be protected from high-speed debris, such as that ejected from a saw or grinding wheel, the safety glasses must be impact resistant and clearly labeled as **ANSI Z87.1** certified. Additionally, safety glasses must incorporate **side shields** to provide extra protection to the eyes from debris entering the eyes from the sides of the face.

If an employee may be exposed to splashing fluids, then **goggles** should be used to protect the eyes. While safety glasses protect from solid debris, tight-fitting goggles provide a seal against the face to prevent **liquids** from entering or dripping into the eyes. Goggles can also be impact rated or have **tinted lenses**, such as for welding, to reduce the risk of eye damage from the radiation emitted while working with a torch.

Face shields provide full face protection and typically consist of a protective barrier attached to a skull cap. The barrier protects from the forehead and can cover the entire face. Face shields protect the face from both fluid and solid objects and can be impact rated or tinted.

HEARING PROTECTION

A hearing protection device is selected according to the amount of noise it can reduce, considering that too much reduction can prevent an employee from hearing alarm indicators or other warnings. There are three main types of **hearing protection devices**:

- **Foam earplugs** are an inexpensive, disposable type of hearing protection. Foam plugs are designed to be inserted into the ear canal and expand to fit the individual. They do not typically interfere with other protective equipment. However, they can be ineffective if not inserted correctly and, if soiled, can introduce dirt into the ear canal.
- **Ear caps** are similar to foam earplugs in their design but are usually attached to a band and are reusable. While earplugs are easily lost, either singly or in pairs, canal caps can be worn around the neck when not in use. Their effectiveness is dependent on the design of the tips and how deep they fit into the ear canal.
- **Earmuffs** differ from plugs and caps in that they are designed to cover the entire outer ear. They are reusable, can be used by multiple employees, and must be properly cleaned and maintained. Earmuffs are also easier to use effectively than plugs or caps. As they are designed to fit over the ear, there is more interpersonal variability in the shape of the head and ears that can impact the effectiveness of the device. Also, the headbands can interfere with other protective equipment, they are less effective when safety glasses are required, and they are much heavier and more cumbersome than plugs or caps.

PROTECTIVE FOOTWEAR

As with all personal protective equipment (PPE), proper **footwear** should be determined based on the hazards expected at the job site. The decision to require work boots versus shoes may be based on the **walking surfaces** the employee will be exposed to. Unstable or movable surfaces would call for the ankle protection provided by boots. **Steel toes** should be selected when tools or materials can fall on the toes or the foot may strike an object. **Steel shanks** should be required when puncture hazards may be present on the floor or ground, such as lumber with nails or screws. Workers doing demo work may need **metatarsal guards** to protect from debris falling on the top of the foot. **Insulated** footwear may be necessary for employees working in cold weather, while gators or boots may be necessary for working in or around water. **Chemical-resistant** boots have specific applications for those who work with large containers of paint, solvents, or other hazardous materials.

HAND PROTECTION

There are numerous choices available for the protection of hands from hazards at a job site. The most commonly selected glove is a leather palm **work glove** which is resistant to friction, provides some cut protection, and is a general purpose glove to protect the hands. Synthetic work gloves may be better suited than leather in cold and wet environments and can incorporate knuckle guards, vibration pads, and textured grip.

Specialty gloves will have applications specific to the hazards a particular task may expose a worker to. Handling sheet metal or wire may necessitate the use of **cut-resistant** gloves like Kevlar-based products. **Welding** gloves are selected based on the type of welding to be performed. **Chemical-resistant** gloves are selected based on the chemicals that are present and how long the employee will be exposed to those chemicals as well as what they will be doing. **Padded** gloves can reduce the vibration that an employee using a jackhammer will experience, which will reduce the chance of nerve damage in the hands. Arc flash **electrical-resistant** gloves are required whenever employees will be working on or near high-voltage equipment.

CHEMICAL PROTECTIVE CLOTHING

In 29 CFR 1910.120, Appendix B, the Occupational Safety and Health Administration classifies chemical clothing **ensembles** in levels from A to D. The system standardizes personal protective equipment (PPE) and aligns the degree of protection with anticipated hazards, with Level D offering the least protection and Level A providing the most.

- **Level D** (nuisance hazards): consists of a "standard" work uniform of shirt, pants, and work boots or safety shoes; may also incorporate the use of coveralls to keep the clothes clean.
- **Level C** (airborne hazards present, but known; skin and eye hazards unlikely): work uniform is used as a base layer; the outer layer includes either an uncoated or coated chemical protective garment; includes an air-purifying respirator; hands are protected by chemical-resistant gloves, one or two pairs (inner and outer pair).
- **Level B** (higher level of respiratory protection): same base layer and elements as Level C, but with the outer chemical-resistant garment being coated and the respiratory protection being a supplied-air system, either a self-contained breathing apparatus (SCBA) or airline respirator.
- **Level A** (highest level of protection, unknown atmospheres, skin-absorbing chemicals, uncontrolled releases): A Level A ensemble is worn underneath a fully-encapsulating suit. Because situations requiring this level of protection are the most hazardous and the equipment is the most complex, employees who will wear Level A equipment are required to have specialized training.

RESPIRATORS

According to the Occupational Safety and Health Administration (OSHA), **inhalation** is the most common route for chemical exposure. Thus, protecting the lungs and airway as well as providing **contaminant-free air** for the body is critical to worker safety. Inhalation hazards include dusts, chemical mists, metal vapors, smoke, toxic gases, asbestos fibers, molds, and fungi.

A **respirator** is a device that provides a barrier between the respiratory system and an atmosphere that contains airborne contaminants. "Respirator" is a broad term that can refer to equipment as simple as a dust mask or as complex as a self-contained breathing apparatus. The two categories of respiratory protection are air-purifying respirators and supplied-air respirators.

- An **air-purifying** respirator removes contaminants from the air that is breathed in by the wearer. The source of air is the surrounding environment, and the contaminants are removed by **filter elements** that are part of the respirator device.
- A **supplied-air respirator (SAR)** is a unit that provides breathing air to the worker. The source of air may be carried by the wearer, such as in a **self-contained breathing apparatus (SCBA)**, or may be attached to a remote air supply, such as **airline respirators.**

Energy Isolation

LOTO

The acronym **LOTO** stands for **lockout/tagout.** LOTO describes a system used to isolate **hazardous energy** to prevent its release while an employee is conducting repair, maintenance, or service activities. When systems have the ability to store electrical, pneumatic, fluid, gravity, mechanical, or chemical energy, that energy has the potential to be released and can cause injury. For example, electrical energy is stored in a circuit, and if an employee is working on that circuit without isolating the energy, there is a risk of shock or electrocution. The energy from gravity is stored by raising a vehicle lift while it is being repaired. A LOTO program uses training, designated roles, positive isolation devices, and informational tags to ensure a system is rendered safe before work occurs.

HAZARDOUS ENERGY TYPES

Hazardous energy is any energy stored in equipment that, if released while an employee is in the area of operation or in contact with the equipment during repair or maintenance, can cause an injury. OSHA identifies seven types of hazardous energy that must be isolated: **electrical, mechanical** (such as springs or blades), **pneumatic** (including compressed gases), **hydraulic** (such as high-pressure water lines or hydraulic fluids under pressure), **chemical** reactions that are in progress, **thermal** energy (including open flames or objects that get hot), and **gravity** (such as lifts and presses). Positive means must be taken to ensure that energy is released from the system or effectively blocked to reduce the risk to employees.

AUTHORIZED EMPLOYEE AND AFFECTED EMPLOYEE

29 CFR 1910.147, OSHA's Control of Hazardous Energy Lockout/Tagout Standard, identifies two classes of employees that are impacted by hazardous energy: authorized employees and affected employees.

Authorized employees are those who have received training on the modes and methods for installing energy isolation devices. They are the individuals who will **perform** the service or maintenance activities on equipment that may have stored energy. Only authorized individuals may apply lockout devices to isolate the energy of a system.

Affected employees are those who **work** on or with equipment that is being serviced or maintained and will require the energy to be isolated. Although they will not be involved in the energy isolation process, they will be impacted when the energy is removed from and returned to the system.

LOCKS AND TAGS

Two types of devices are typically used to control the release of hazardous energy during repairs and maintenance: locks and tags.

A **lockout device** ("lock") uses a **positive means** to hold an energy isolation device (such as a clamp, release, shutoff switch, or valve cover) in a safe position. The device is controlled by a key or combination and should only be removed by the person who placed the device. The devices, typically versions of a padlock, must be dedicated to controlling hazardous energy, durable enough for the environment in which they are used, and uniquely identifiable.

A **tagout device** ("tag") is a warning sign that indicates the equipment shall not be operated until such time as the tag is removed by the individual who placed it on the energy isolation device.

REQUIREMENTS

A **tagout device** (or "tag") is attached to the energy-isolating device to prevent accidental startup or energy release during servicing, maintenance, and repair activities on equipment and systems that can store hazardous energy. Per 29 CFR 1910.147, the tag must be **non-reusable, durable, weather resistant**, able to **withstand** 50 pounds of force, and have the following information:

- The **name** of the employee applying the device
- A **warning statement,** such as "do not start," "do not close," or "do not operate"

PROTECTING FROM AN ARC FLASH HAZARD

When employees must work on **high-voltage** systems that are not de-energized, they must use specialized personal protective equipment to prevent injury. The most common mode of injury is by way of an arc flash. An **arc flash** is when the electricity jumps from the equipment across the air void to a nearby conductor, which, during repair or maintenance activities, is the employee.

In these instances, the worker must wear personal protective equipment (PPE) properly **rated** for the amount of energy the worker may be exposed to. The **ensemble** includes face protection, body protection, and hand protection. The face is protected by a tinted **visor and hood**. The body is protected by an **insulated suit**. The worker also uses rubber **insulated gloves.** Since the hands are closest to the equipment, the gloves must be in good condition and must be tested twice per year, per 29 CFR 1910.137.

Audits, Inspections, or Evaluations

INSPECTION

A safety **inspection** is a formal or informal process wherein the safety professional conducts a **walk-through** of the workplace to identify hazards. An inspection may be focused on behaviors (are employees adhering to safe work practices), equipment (are the fire extinguishers in good condition), or systems (are the safety data sheet binders up to date). The items evaluated during an inspection may come from written procedures, standards, regulations, or manufacturer's recommendations. Any hazards or deficiencies that are identified should be addressed or an **action plan** developed to reduce the associated risk.

AUDITS VS. INSPECTIONS

While an inspection may be either formal or informal, **audits** are typically formal evaluations of adherence to **written procedures**. While inspection items may be derived from best practices, manufacturer's recommendations, or written programs, audits are directed by an organization's documents. An audit will evaluate whether the business is following its own written policies and procedures.

Inspections are based on observations, and audits are based on **records**. An auditor will review inspection logs, maintenance records, and training rosters to determine whether the business has proof that it is complying with its formal policies. The final product of an audit should be a report for **management** and staff regarding where the system is performing well and where **corrective action** needs to be taken. Inspection results are typically provided to the impacted stakeholders as a means of identifying hazards and requesting corrective actions.

AUDIT FINDINGS

An audit evaluates a system's adherence to written policies and procedures. If a system, such as a safety management system, is found deficient or not meeting a requirement, it is labeled a "**finding**" or "deficiency." ISO standards will list elements as required, desired, and optional. In a formal audit scenario, there are four types of findings. Listed in order of most to least severe, a deficiency or finding can be qualified as:

- **Condition adverse to quality**—this type of finding means that a required element is not present or is not functioning as intended, and a negative impactful result, such as an injury or fatality, can occur
- **Condition not adverse to quality**—typically associated with missing or non-functional desired, but not mandatory, elements; although the result would still be negative, the result is typically less severe, such as first aid or a near miss

- **Observations**—an observation is an optional element of a program that is noted as missing where its inclusion could improve the functionality of the system
- **Opportunities for improvement**—areas where the program is found not to be deficient or missing an element but could be modified to be more effective

INITIATION OF OSHA INSPECTIONS

An **OSHA inspector** has the legal authority to inspect any worksite. They may conduct an inspection as the result of a **reported injury**, due to a **complaint** about the worksite, or as part of a **planned** rotation of inspections, referred to as programmed inspections.

The OSHA inspector is not required to notify the employer prior to the inspection. They must present their **credentials** prior to accessing the site, formally **announce** their reason for the inspection, and should not be denied or otherwise inhibited from conducting an inspection. If the work location has employee groups, they may accompany the inspector as well as an employer representative. The employer representative does not need to be a manager or a safety professional.

SAFETY VIOLATION

In most instances, whenever a **safety violation** is identified during an inspection or evaluation, the supervisor or safety professional should stop the task as soon as possible. The situation must be pointed out to those involved, the proper method should be conveyed or demonstrated, and only then should work be allowed to continue. Only if stopping the task would create a safety risk should any correction be delayed. Waiting until the next scheduled meeting or until a formal report has been filed will not result in the desired change in behavior.

Incident Investigations, Documentation, and Corrective Action

FACT-FINDING VS. FAULT-FINDING INCIDENT INVESTIGATIONS

The goal of an **incident investigation** is to determine the **factors** that led to an injury or illness so it can be prevented from happening again. The investigator must determine the **conditions or actions** that resulted in the negative outcome. Depending on the culture of the organization, such an investigation can look to establish fault or establish facts.

In a **fault-finding** mindset, the investigator is looking to assign blame for the incident. They are looking for a responsible individual—the person who placed the cord in the walkway that tripped the employee who fell and broke their arm. The end goal is typically **punitive** in nature, resulting in discipline for the individual who created the hazardous condition. The downside of fault-finding is that even though the person identified as "responsible" may be removed from the environment, the circumstances that allowed the condition to occur are usually not resolved. For example, if the individual who left the cord in the walkway is removed from the workplace, the lack of training on proper cord management or the absence of a cable crossover is not addressed. Thus, the circumstances remain, and an injury is likely to recur.

In a **fact-finding** investigation, the investigator is trying to determine **why** something happened. The individual action is just the logical end to a series of events that resulted in an injury. If the investigator focuses on the "why" and can determine the **root cause**, then the underlying conditions can truly be addressed and the risk reduced if not eliminated completely. This approach is a higher-level, more systems view of health and safety.

JOB SITE INJURIES AND ILLNESSES

The Occupational Safety and Health Administration (OSHA) 29 CFR Part 1904 requires that any employer with more than ten (10) employees keep a **log** of any **serious injuries**. Recording an injury does not imply fault on the part of the employee or employer, nor that a violation of an OSHA standard occurred.

An employer must record any injury, illness, or death that is **work-related**. To be work-related, the injury must have occurred as a result of a task assigned by a supervisor or a pre-existing condition that was **aggravated** by a task assigned by a supervisor. Employers must record their injuries using an OSHA 300, 300-A, and 301 forms or equivalents. The 300-A log is an annual summary of all recordable injuries and must be **posted** at the worksite from February 1 through April 30 of the following year.

RECORDABLE

The Occupational Safety and Health Administration (OSHA) requires that logs of recordable injuries and illnesses be maintained by the employer. Per OSHA, a recordable injury or illness is work-related and

- results in **death** (any injury or illness that results in death must be reported to OSHA within eight (8) hours of the employer's knowledge),
- results in **days away from work** (the start for the count of days away from work begins the day after the injury occurred),
- results in days of **restricted work or transfer** to another job,
- requires **medical treatment** beyond first aid, or
- results in a loss of consciousness.

All recordable injuries and illnesses must be recorded on an OSHA 300 log or equivalent.

OSHA FORMS 300 AND 300-A

The Occupational Safety and Health Administration (OSHA) requires that work-related injuries are **recorded and reported** using forms 300 and 300-A or forms that record the same information as the OSHA forms. Such recordkeeping is used to direct the health and safety program for an employer by identifying locations or activities that need better control methods implemented.

The OSHA 300 form is the **Log of Work-Related Injuries and Illnesses**. The log contains a brief description of each injury and illness that occurred during a **single calendar year**. **Privacy cases** (those involving injuries to sensitive areas, reproductive organs, sexual assault, mental illness, communicable diseases [such as HIV, tuberculosis, or hepatitis], needlesticks, or other cases where the employee requests privacy) are exempted from the disclosure of identifying information.

The OSHA 300-A form is the **annual summary** of all work-related injuries and illnesses. The form records the same cases as OSHA 300 but does not contain the same level of detail. The 300-A form must be certified by an employer representative and must be **posted** in a visible location at the worksite from February 1 through April 30 of the following year.

RECORDABLE VS. REPORTABLE INJURY OR ILLNESS

The Occupational Safety and Health Administration (OSHA) requires that employers maintain a record of all work-related injuries that meet certain criteria, termed **recordable** injuries. A recordable injury or illness is one that requires more than first aid treatment or results in death, days lost from work, restricted work or job transfer, or a loss of consciousness.

However, OSHA also requires the employer notify their local OSHA office for certain injuries and illnesses, termed **reportable**. The employer must contact OSHA within **eight (8) hours** of an employee **death**. The employer must also contact OSHA within **twenty-four (24) hours** of any work-related injury or illness that results in an in-person **hospitalization** of one or more employees, **loss of an eye**, or **amputation**. OSHA has determined that amputation refers to any loss of bone.

Thus, where all reportable injuries and illnesses are recordable, not all recordable illnesses and injuries are reportable.

INCIDENT INVESTIGATION

A rapid and methodical approach to health and safety incidents is critical in identifying and correcting root causes. As soon as medical aid is rendered and the victim has been removed, the **incident investigation** should start.

The first step is to **secure** the incident site. Similar to a crime scene investigation, people moving in and out of the incident location can obscure and destroy, either intentionally or unintentionally, evidence of how and why the incident occurred. Keeping unnecessary personnel out of the location preserves the scene.

Next, evidence must be **identified and preserved**. The most difficult part of an investigation is identifying what is relevant to the incident. Identifying and preserving important information is critical to identifying the root cause. Evidence must be recorded and preserved to help tell the story of what happened and why.

Witnesses must be identified and questioned as quickly as possible to make sure their recollection is accurate. Witnesses can be interviewed in a neutral location or asked to reenact events at the incident site. Interview as many witnesses as possible to obtain a complete and accurate picture of the sequence of events.

Finally, a **report** must be completed to document the results of the investigation and make any **recommendations** for corrections. The report can be used to convey findings to management and could be used in any future court proceedings.

ROOT CAUSE ANALYSIS

The purpose of an accident investigation is to identify the **root cause** to prevent future occurrences. A root cause is defined as the **fundamental reason** that something happened. It is that thing that, if changed, would have resulted in a different outcome. A **root cause analysis** is a method used to identify the fundamental reason an incident occurred. There are numerous **formal processes** (fault tree analysis, failure modes analysis, fishbone diagrams, etc.) to assist in identifying the root cause. Direct and indirect causes may be uncovered during the process. Causes can be categorized as equipment, environment, personnel, and management. Once a root cause has been identified, a corrective action can be implemented to prevent the incident from happening in the future.

LESSONS LEARNED REVIEW

After an emergency incident or an evacuation drill, stakeholders should be assembled for a **lessons learned** session. In this session, the event is reviewed from each contributor's experience and what they observed. The goals are to **identify successes** that can continue or be leveraged in other areas as well as **failures** that need to be addressed. Although not part of a continual improvement program which seeks to make incremental advances for a particular safety program, lessons learned are geared more toward solving practical problems that arose during the event. For example, an emergency evacuation plan may be effective in getting people out of a building in a short period of time, but consideration was not given to the inability of such a large group of people to use the sidewalk. Another example could be identifying the need for extra pens and batteries for the incident command group—not a failure of the program, but more of a practical problem that was unanticipated.

CAPA

CAPA is an acronym for **corrective action/preventive action**. A **corrective action** is a plan that describes who will address a hazard that has been identified, what the desired state should be, what actions will be taken, and how much time will be required to implement the correction. A **preventive action** identifies the same information but in relation to a potential future hazardous condition. In an example where an employee slips on leaking machine oil from a nearby conveyor and breaks their arm, the corrective action would be to clean up the oil spill, while the preventive action would be to fix the leaking machine. A corrective action fixes the hazard; a preventive action prevents it from occurring again.

Safety and Health Hazards

Hazards Associated with Working Around Pressurized Systems

SAFE PRESSURE LIMIT FOR COMPRESSED AIR

Air compressors have the capability of providing a range of pressures depending on the end use. Most air hand tools require a pressure between 70-90 psi while larger tools may require up to 120 psi. Most piped systems in buildings provide a pressure of around 100 psi. Portable compressors can produce air pressures up to or exceeding 175 psi.

High-pressure air used for cleaning can also kick up dirt and debris, creating a risk for eye injuries. In order to reduce this risk, OSHA has set a limit of **30 psi** for compressed air that is used for cleaning. Under no circumstances should an employee used compressed air to clean their clothing, due to the hazards to the eyes and respiratory system.

PRESSURE VESSELS

Pressure vessels are sealed containers designed to hold materials (gases or liquids) above or below **atmospheric pressure**. Systems used to deliver materials, such as pipes and hoses, may also be pressurized. The pressure may exceed the surrounding pressure ("high pressure") or may be less than the ambient pressure ("low pressure"). High pressure is created by compressing the fluid or gas within the container or system. Air compressors, boilers, and gas delivery lines all operate under high pressure. Low-pressure systems are created by way of vacuum systems removing air from the system. Vessels under high or low pressure can fail, resulting in injury-producing projectiles as well as the release of the contents from the system.

HAZARDS ASSOCIATED WITH HIGH-PRESSURE VESSELS

OSHA identifies a **pressure vessel** as one that operates at pressures greater than 15 psig (pounds per square inch gauge). Certain pieces of equipment are considered high-pressure vessels, such as gas storage tanks and boilers. If these vessels have cracks or are otherwise damaged, they can fail, sometimes catastrophically. Such a failure would result in the release of the **contents** as well as the **physical hazard** of either fragments of the container or the entire container itself becoming a **projectile**. Injuries can include cuts, fractures, and contusions. In the case of boilers or other high-temperature vessels, there is the additional hazard of burns to exposed skin and eyes.

In addition to the physical hazard, high-pressure vessels may contain hazardous materials. Upon container failure, the substance itself is released and employees are **exposed.** Flammable, corrosive, or toxic gases or fluids may be ejected over large distances, increasing the risk of fire or exposure to those impacted by the release.

FLUIDS OR GASES PENETRATING THE SKIN

Gases or fluids may be stored or used at **high pressure**. Pressure is used to move fluids through piping systems or to use the produced force to do work, such as in a hydraulic lift. Hydraulic fluids can operate between 2,000 to 3,000 psi, with an internationally accepted maximum pressure around 10,000 psi. Compressed gas cylinders are pressurized, on average, to 2,000 psi.

The hazard presented by high-pressure systems is that any pressure over **100 psi** can **penetrate** the skin. This means that an employee who is exposed to pressures exceeding that value may experience an injection exposure. In an **injection**, the substance pierces the skin and is deposited between skin and muscle, forming a pocket. If the substance is corrosive or toxic, the injury can be extensive. Even the injection of air under the skin will cause painful injuries.

Hazards Associated with Walking/Working Surfaces

WALKING/WORKING SURFACE

The Occupational Safety and Health Administration (OSHA) defines a walking/working surface as any horizontal or vertical surface that an employee will pass over or through, work on, or use to gain access to a work location. This definition applies to nearly every surface, unless otherwise excluded by a standard, that an employee may encounter. **Walking surfaces** include ramps, stairs, ladders, and walkways. **Working surfaces** include roofs, scaffolds, and floors.

HAZARDS

Slips, trips, and falls (STFs) are responsible for up to 25% of all workplace injuries and are the primary hazard associated with walking and working surfaces. STFs can occur on wet or icy surfaces and can be caused by objects in the walkway, such as cords or crumpled mats, or uneven walking surfaces. Distracted walking, running, and stair climbing are also categorized as STF hazards. Improper cord management, lack of attention to housekeeping, and poor sidewalk maintenance are all contributing factors to STF incidents. Injuries from STFs can include abrasions, contusions, dislocations, and fractures.

HOLES

OSHA defines a **hole** as any opening in a floor, roof, or other walking surface that is at least **two (2) inches in the smallest dimension**. A hole can be a defect in a sidewalk, a gap in a ramp, a missing roof tile, or an improperly seated manhole cover. Holes can cause **tripping hazards** resulting in falls or can cause **fractures** to feet or toes that get caught in the hole. Tools and materials can fall through larger holes, striking those working or walking on levels below.

All holes must be **covered, guarded,** or otherwise visually **identified** to prevent individuals from getting a foot, toe, or shoe caught in them, which can result in a same-level fall injury.

COEFFICIENT OF FRICTION

Friction is used to describe the interaction of two surfaces that are moving past each other. It assigns a value to the degree of **sliding** or motion that occurs when the two surfaces interact. In occupational safety, the **coefficient of friction** is applied to walking surfaces to describe the **grip** a shoe has to a particular surface.

The coefficient of friction has a value between 0 and 1, where 0 means the two surfaces have absolutely no interaction or grip ("slippery") and 1 means the two surfaces will stick to each other and not release ("bound"). Values **below 0.1** are typically considered "slippery" when used to describe the grip of a shoe. It is recommended that walking surfaces have a coefficient of friction of at least 0.5 to reduce the risk of slipping and falling. For example, a leather-soled shoe may have a coefficient of friction with dry vinyl of 0.6, but if the vinyl becomes wet, the value drops to 0.004.

Hazards Associated with Working at Heights

IMPLEMENTING FALL PROTECTION CONTROL MEASURES

For general industry, an employer is required to implement **fall protection** controls when employees will be working at any elevation where they will be exposed to an unprotected side that is **four (4) feet or more** above the next level. However, ramps or walkways that are more than **thirty (30) inches** high must have a protective system, such as guardrails, to prevent falls to the lower level. For example, employees who work on loading docks where the truck bay is lower than the dock plate by more than four (4) feet must have a fall protection system in place when trucks are not present.

HAZARDS ASSOCIATED WITH WORKING AT HEIGHTS

There are two primary hazards associated with working at heights—falling and falling objects. Unprotected workers can **fall**, which can result in injury or death. Falling from a catwalk, loading dock, or an observation walkway above a machine can result in contusions, fractures, puncture wounds, or head trauma, depending on the height of the fall and the surface the worker lands on. Secondly, **objects** that are dropped from an elevated location onto a path where workers travel can strike the workers below. Dropping a tool, supplies, or materials onto a passerby on a lower level can injure the head, resulting in cuts, bruises, fractures, or even death.

PREVENT INJURIES FROM FALLING OBJECTS

Objects that fall from one level to another can cause major injuries when they strike someone working or walking below and can even result in death. The risk of **objects falling** from heights and striking workers below can be reduced by the installation of toeboards, the use of canopies, or by deploying barricades.

A **toeboard** is a raised barrier at floor level that is installed at or near the unprotected edge to prevent objects from getting pushed, kicked, or otherwise falling off the edge. An employer may opt to erect **canopies** above the walking path on a lower level to catch or divert falling objects—the canopy provides a protective "roof" for those passing or working underneath. Another option is for the employer to establish **fall zones** by using barricades or fencing to keep employees out of the area where falling objects from upper levels may land. This provides a designated area where materials can be thrown or dropped from higher levels a safe distance from pedestrian traffic.

TOEBOARDS

A **toeboard** is a raised edge that is used to prevent tools or materials from being knocked over the edge onto a lower level. As implied by the name, toeboards are attached to the floor or edge of the working surface. Toeboards must be at least 3 ½ inches tall and may not have a **gap** between the bottom and the surface that is greater than ¼ inch. If tools and materials are piled higher than the toeboard used as part of a guardrail system, **netting or sheeting** must be installed from the top of the toeboard to the midrail or top rail, depending on the height of the stack.

Hazards Associated with Elevated Work Platforms

ELEVATED WORK PLATFORM

An **elevated work platform** is a **mobile** device that has a work surface that is **adjustable** in height. The platform may be motorized or simply have wheels allowing the device to be moved to work locations. The platform may be manually adjustable in both height and location, such as in the case of **mobile scaffold** systems, or may be motorized. The most familiar types of **motorized** elevated work platforms are **scissor lifts** that extend in the vertical plane carrying workers and materials, or **boom lifts** that can telescope, lift, and rotate the basket which contains the workers.

FALL HAZARDS

The two fall hazards associated with elevated work platforms are **falling people** and **falling objects**. Even though scissor lifts are typically outfitted with guardrail systems and fall protection devices are not required, it is not uncommon to find workers sitting or standing on the rails or using ladders improperly to increase the effective height of the device. This greatly increases the risk of falling from height and the severity of the related injury. Boom lifts may jerk, jolt, or rotate if the controls are accidentally actuated, resulting in the worker being ejected from the basket.

The other hazard associated with elevated work platforms is **falling objects**. Objects can be intentionally or unintentionally dropped, kicked, or otherwise fall from the platform, where they can strike a person on the ground, causing injury or death. Falling bricks, scrap material, or a dropped tool can strike someone on the head, resulting in a severe injury.

ADDITIONAL HAZARDS

By their design and intent, **elevated work platforms** are used for personnel to work at heights. However, as the device increases in height, the center of mass of the unit also rises, increasing the risk of **tip-overs**. If the work platform is unbalanced or is raised too high, typically considered more than **four times** higher than the base is wide, the risk of the entire unit tipping over increases. Additionally, overhead hazards such as electrical lines or overhangs, that are normally well above ground, can impact elevated platforms. If the platform or an employee touches a live electrical wire, there is a chance of **shock** or even electrocution. Overhangs can pin a worker against the platform, resulting in **caught-between** injuries, that can be fatal.

Hazards Associated with Ladders

FALLS FROM LADDERS

The primary hazard associated with ladders is **falling**. Worker familiarity with ladders may cause a degree of complacency and a loss of respect for the height the ladder provides. Even the most experienced worker can fall from a ladder due to improper securing, improper use, lack of maintenance, or overloading.

Ladders that are not **properly secured** or are placed on uneven ground can be unstable such that a slight shift in weight or body position can cause the ladder and the worker to fall. **Improper use** includes using a ladder of insufficient height for the job, leaning a self-supporting ladder against a surface as if it were an extension ladder, not extending the ladder high enough above the next level, or stacking ladders on one another to increase the effective height. Ladders that are not properly **maintained** and have cracked rungs or rails can fail unexpectedly during use, causing a fall. Workers may not realize that each ladder is rated with a maximum load for safe use. The rating includes the weight of the worker plus materials and, if **overloaded**, the ladder may fail or topple, resulting in a fall injury.

SELECTING A CORRECTLY SIZED LADDER

The American Ladder Institute has identified the most common mistake associated with ladder use as selecting a ladder of **incorrect height**. Ladders that are **too short** will often result in the user overreaching, standing on the top cap or first step, or seeking improper ways to increase the effective height such as placing supports under the feet of the ladder. A-frame ladders that are too tall may seem low risk until the user realizes the amount of space required to fully extend the spreaders. In this instance, the user may opt to improperly collapse the A-frame and lean the ladder against the workspace, also resulting in an imbalanced and unsecure footing. Extension ladders that are too short will not reach the work level, and ones that are too long increase the risk of toppling.

METAL LADDERS

If an employee uses a ladder to work on or near live **electrical circuits**, only fiberglass or wood ladders are allowed to be used. **Metal ladders**, which are in contact with the ground, can become part of the **circuit** if they or the employee contact a live wire or damaged cord. This contact can result in a shock or electrocution. Even mild shocks can cause an impulsive reaction to let go of the ladder, resulting in a fall and the associated injuries.

RUNGS OF A LADDER

The **rungs** of a ladder are the horizontal members used for **climbing**. Both the hands and the feet will make contact with the rungs during ascension and descension. If the rungs are cracked, weakened, or overloaded, they can **fail**, resulting in a fall. Both wood and metal ladders can **splinter**, causing cuts or puncture wounds to a hand or a foot. In wet weather or when oily products are being applied, the rungs can become **slippery** also resulting in a fall injury.

Hazards Associated with Industrial Lifting Vehicles

INDUSTRIAL LIFT VEHICLES IN MOTION

The most common industrial lift vehicle is a **forklift**, a motorized vehicle used to lift and transport materials. Often used in vehicle docks to load and unload materials, the forklift is typically smaller than other nearby vehicles. This can put the forklift in a situation where it can be **struck by** other larger vehicles, particularly when vehicles have large blind spots and are unable to clearly see in all directions. Loading operations also involve a pedestrian-vehicle interface where the forklift can **strike** pedestrians as it rounds corners, backs up, or moves with a load that obscures the vision of the driver. Loading docks often have elevated platforms, which present the hazard of a forklift **falling** into the vehicle bay or **overturning** as it drives from one location to another, which has been identified by the National Institute of Occupational Safety and Health as the most common hazard associated with forklifts.

LOADS OF INDUSTRIAL LIFT VEHICLES

Using **industrial lift vehicles** such as forklifts to move materials eliminates the risk of injury that can be caused by manual lifting. Additionally, large loads, heavy loads, and a lot of material can be moved at one time as opposed to manual material movement. However, precautions must be taken to reduce the hazards associated with using equipment to move loads, which include:

- **Unstable** or **off-center loads** can fall off the vehicle or cause the forklift to tip over.
- Exceeding the **load limit** for the equipment can result in a dropped load or damage to the vehicle.
- Blocked, uneven, or otherwise compromised **routes of travel** for the vehicle can cause the load or vehicle to become unstable, increasing the risk of a dropped load or toppled vehicle.

UNTRAINED FORKLIFT DRIVERS

Forklifts and other industrial lift vehicles can present several hazards if put in the hands of an untrained driver. Motorized lift vehicles are rated for specific **load**

limits and must be **loaded correctly** to prevent tipping over. Handling a forklift, especially around pedestrians and other vehicles, can be hazardous due the **limited visibility** and tight spaces these vehicles operate in. The proper use of **controls**, adequately warning others of the vehicle's presence, awareness of the **limited visibility** while operating the vehicle, and proper **inspection and maintenance** of the vehicle are necessary to avoid accidents. Due to these and other hazards, OSHA requires **training** for any person before they use an industrial lift vehicle (per 29 CFR 1910.178) as well as a skills test to demonstrate they can handle the vehicle safely.

INDUSTRIAL LIFT VEHICLES

In addition to the hazards related to loads and the risks presented to pedestrians, industrial lift vehicles such as **forklifts** can present an environmental hazard under certain conditions. Forklifts are powered by engines which may be powered by electricity, natural gas, or fossil fuel. If the forklift used inside of a warehouse uses a gas-powered engine, the toxic **combustion by-products** produced by the engine can accumulate and present a hazard to workers inside the building. The presence of multiple vehicles increases the magnitude and risk of carbon monoxide, NOX, and other emissions negatively impacting the health of the operator and warehouse personnel.

Hazards Associated with Hand and Power Tools

HAND TOOLS

A **hand tool** is any tool that is **manually operated**. Hand tools include hammers, chisels, screwdrivers, wrenches, axes, and shovels. Hand tools are very common at most workplaces. While many people are comfortable with using some type of hand tool, this complacency often results in a failure to recognize the hazards they present. Ejected debris, noise, soft tissue injuries, and cuts are common injuries caused by hand tools.

Hand tools can **eject** small pieces of debris that can enter the eyes or even pierce the skin, while large pieces of debris pose struck-by hazards that can cause bruises or cuts. Using tools on metal or working in small spaces can expose the worker to potentially dangerous levels of **occupational noise**. **Soft tissue injuries**, which include muscle strains and ligament or tendon sprains, can result when a hand tool breaks, slips from the point of use, or when workers overexert themselves while working. Tools with blades or teeth can **cut** or pierce the skin—sharp tools can easily penetrate clothing and skin, while dull bladed or toothed tools require additional force which can cause the tool to slip, cutting the employee.

CAUSES OF HAZARDS

The two main causes of hazards presented by hand tools are **misuse** and **improper maintenance**. If an employee uses a wrench as a hammer, the mouth of the wrench could break off, creating a projectile, or the mouth may become distorted, which will present a hazard when tightening bolts. Hand tools should only be used for their intended purpose—use the right tool for the job.

Improper maintenance increases the risk of injury caused by hand tools. Splintered or cracked handles can cause lacerations or puncture injuries to the hand. Loose handles or tool heads can result in the head flying off the handle and striking the user or a passerby.

POWER TOOLS

A **power tool** is any tool that executes a task using a **motor or drive**. Power tools include drills, grinding wheels, and reciprocating saws. Tools may be **powered** by air (pneumatic), electricity, or gas. Similar to hand tools, **power tools** expose employees to the risks of ejected debris, occupational noise, and soft tissue damage. However, power tools have the additional hazards associated with their power source.

Power tools by their design deliver more power to the work task. Thus, they have a higher risk associated with **ejected debris**, may create larger pieces of debris compared to a hand tool, and the debris will have more energy when displaced, which can result in a more serious injury to the worker or passersby. There is also an increased risk of occupational **noise** exposure from the drive system of the tool. With the increase in power, there is an increased demand on the worker's body to **control** the tool and a higher risk of the hand slipping, which can lead to **muscle injuries** or sprains.

The tool's power **source** presents additional hazards. Electrical power cords can become frayed or damaged, posing the risk of an electric **shock**. Pneumatic tools use **compressed air** at high pressure—air pressurized above 100 psi can break the skin. Gas-powered tools introduce a **flammability** hazard of the fuel to power the tool as well as expelling hazardous exhaust gases.

POWDER-ACTUATED TOOLS

Powder-actuated tools use a process similar to firearms to drive fasteners into hard materials like concrete and steel. The cartridge contains a primer and powder that, when struck by the firing pin, cause a small explosion that either acts on a piston (**low velocity**) or on the fastener itself (**high velocity**). Powder-actuated tools can be used in tighter spaces than a drill and require fewer steps to install the fastener, where a drill requires boring, insertion of a threaded plug, and then the fastener. powder-actuated tool can either be a trigger-initiated nail gun or require a hammer to discharge the cartridge, such as a ramset.

Because the process of installing the fastener uses a powder charge, these tools cannot be used in flammable atmospheres as they can act as a **source of ignition**. If a powder-actuated tool is used on brittle materials such as tile, it can cause extensive damage to the material, including **ejecting** pieces into the air. Using a powder-actuated tool on materials that are too soft, such as drywall, can result in the projectile **penetrating** the material, coming out on the other side at a high velocity. The discharge of the cartridge is loud, and workers should use hearing protection for the **noise** hazard. Ejected materials from the fastener can pose a risk to the **eyes** if the employee is not wearing safety glasses. Powder tools require specifically treated fasteners due to the velocity of the fastener and the hardness of the materials typically used. Employees should be **trained** on the safe use of the tool prior to being allowed to use it at the job site.

Hazards Associated with Working Around Moving Parts and Pinch Points

MACHINE AREAS CAUSING INJURIES

Machines leverage **mechanical power** to conduct work with a force or speed that exceeds the capabilities of a person. In order to execute such work, the machine uses **power** to flatten, mix, cut, press, form, or stretch materials. Within any machine, there are numerous **moving parts** to complete any task. A machine can be separated into three distinct hazardous areas which can cause injuries:

- **Point of operation**—this is the part of the machine where the **work** is done, such as the cutting blade, mixer, calendar rollers, or press plates.
- **Power transmission apparatus**—this part of the machine **transfers** the energy from the drive system to the point of operation. It may be an axle, gear system, or piston that moves, gradually or suddenly, to operate the machine.
- **Other moving parts**—this can include raw material input locations, intermediate product transfers (from one process step to another), finishing steps, and final product removal from the process. Hazards include robot arms, pulleys, conveyor belts, and packaging devices.

PINCH POINT

A **pinch point** is a specific hazard associated with moving machinery that is created when two moving objects come together. Pinch points are usually identified as areas where the moving pieces come into **contact** with one another or the space between them **narrows**. Examples of pinch points include conveyor belts (where the moving wheel meets the belt), rollers, and gear systems.

Pinch points are particularly hazardous because once clothing, hair, jewelry, or a body part is caught by the moving parts, it is difficult to remove them.

MACHINE MOTIONS CAUSING INJURIES

The **motion** of a moving machine can be classified into one of three general categories: rotating, reciprocating, and transverse.

- A **rotating** motion is when a portion of the machine moves around a **single axis**. Machines can rotate in a single direction or have components that move in opposite directions. This motion is found in rollers, mixers, and flywheels.

- **Reciprocating motion** is a back-and-forth or up-and-down repeated motion, such as with a blade, press, or loom.
- **Transverse motion** is movement in a continuous straight line. Belts and pulley systems can be described as transverse systems.

PINCH POINT INJURIES

Pinch point injuries are caused when a body part is caught or pulled into an area where one object is **moving** past another. For example, the area where a conveyor belt contacts a roller is a pinch point. Due to the reduction in clearance between the moving parts, crushing-type injuries can result, as well as the potential for amputation or, in extreme cases, death. Inattention, loose items, ineffective guards, and reaching into moving equipment are all causes of pinch point injuries.

Pinch point injuries can be caused by an employee's **inattention**. Not being aware of their environment can result in an employee inadvertently placing their hand or foot near a moving part where it could get caught and pulled into the pinch point. Wearing **loose clothing** (especially gloves), long hair, or loose jewelry can result in these items getting caught by moving parts, pulling the worker into the pinch point. **Machine guards** that are removed, inadequate, or in poor condition may not properly protect an employee from the pinch point hazard. Guards are installed to protect from injury and should always be intact and in place before using the equipment. Finally, any employee who reaches into **operating machinery** to adjust materials, clear a jam, or make an adjustment to the machine is risking a pinch point injury.

BODY PART MOST FREQUENTLY INJURED

The body part most frequently injured by **pinch points** is the **hand**, including fingers. People will often place their hands on or near moving parts to clear a jam, to perform an operation they believe can be done quickly, or by simply not paying attention to where they rest their hands. **Gloves** should be avoided around any moving parts as the loose material or glove fingers can get caught, pulling the finger or entire hand into the danger zone. Hand injuries include cuts, fractures, "degloving" where the skin is pulled from the hand or finger, and amputations. Additionally, loose clothing or dangling bracelets can get caught in the moving parts, resulting in the worker's fingers, hand, arm, or body being pulled into the pinch point. In extreme circumstances where the body is pulled into the pinch points, a fatality can result.

Hazards Associated with Poor Housekeeping

HOUSEKEEPING

When used in relation to workplace safety, **housekeeping** refers to not only keeping areas clean but also to removing clutter and debris that can create **tripping** or **fire hazards**. Whenever possible, walkways, stairways, and floors should remain clear of materials, tools, scrap, and debris. Hoses, cords, and lines can present tripping hazards, while raw materials or finished product can clutter a walkway, not only making walking dangerous but also impeding any emergency exit paths. Unwanted scrap, packaging, or wrapping should be placed in proper **waste containers** to reduce the amount of fuel available in the event of a spark or fire.

BIOLOGICAL HAZARDS

Housekeeping refers to the process of maintaining a workspace clutter-free and in an organized condition. When scrap, debris, garbage, or waste is allowed to accumulate, these areas can provide **hiding** or **breeding** spaces for vermin, insects, and other pests. Discarded food can be a **nutrition source**, while the spaces between and among clutter provide **nesting** spaces for the pests. If moisture or food wastes are present, poor housekeeping can provide conditions ripe for **mold and fungi** growth. Airborne spores or toxic waste products can be harmful to employees, resulting in illnesses or allergic reactions.

PHYSICAL HAZARDS

A cluttered and messy worksite can present several physical hazards to employees. Tools, cords, hoses, and excess materials left lying around can cause someone to **trip and fall**, resulting in sprains, strains, bruises, or even fractures. Piles of unwanted materials may hide electrical wires or circuits which can **shock** an employee. Unwanted scrap lumber or sheet metal can create a **cut** or **puncture** hazard if someone steps on the nails or screws left in the materials.

Hazards Associated with Hot Work

HOT WORK

Hot work is described by the Occupational Safety and Health Administration in the construction fire prevention standard (29 CFR 1910.252) as any activity that generates sparks, heat, or slag. These activities include **welding, cutting,** and **heating** of metal objects. The National Fire Protection Association (NFPA 51B) defines hot work as any operation that involves **burning** or **welding** that has the potential to start a fire. Other types of hot work include brazing, soldering, grinding, or drilling of metals.

PRIMARY HAZARD

Hot work, which is any activity that produces sparks, heat, or slag, is a very hazardous activity. The sparks, heat, and slag that are generated can be **sources of ignition** for flammable and combustible materials such as paper, wood, or solvents. Depending on the nearby sources of fuel, the hot work can generate enough heat to ignite some materials, even when transferred through objects such as metal walls, pipes, or fixtures.

Hot work activities can be hazardous not only in the space the work is occurring in but also in adjacent spaces. Hot work on floors, walls, and ceilings can introduce sparks or slag that can pass through cracks, holes, or defects into these adjacent spaces, which can ignite fuels located in these areas.

DESIGNATED VS. PERMIT-REQUIRED HOT WORK AREAS

The National Fire Prevention Association (NFPA) Standard 51B identifies two areas where hot work can be performed—a designated area and a permit-required area.

A **designated hot work area** is a permanent location that is dedicated to hot work. The area is outfitted with non-combustible surfaces, is maintained fire-safe, and properly contains all sparks or slag that may be generated during the work. The area may be plumbed with local **exhaust ventilation** to remove welding fumes from the employee's breathing zone. Designated areas require a **permit** from the local fire authority which must be renewed annually.

Permit-required hot work areas are any **temporary** locations where hot work will occur. The area must be rendered safe prior to work and must be monitored for at least thirty (30) minutes after the work is finished to make sure that any embers do not start a fire.

WELDING VENTILATION

Ventilation refers to both the process of bringing fresh air into a space and the process of removing airborne contaminants from an area. Ventilation systems are more effective when they are **mechanical**, using blowers and fans to provide more air exchanges in any given period of time. **General ventilation** refers to the process of bringing fresh air into an area. Outside air is forced into a space, which causes the contaminated air to be forced out. **Local exhaust ventilation** refers to a focused process where a duct or other collector is placed as close to the work as possible and pulls metal fumes out of the work area.

Mechanical ventilation is required for welding that occurs in **confined spaces** or any welding that involves metals or flux that contains **lead, zinc, cadmium**, or **chromium**. Welding and cutting operations in these situations can result in long-term health problems if the fumes are inhaled. Therefore, mechanical ventilation systems are required to reduce or eliminate the presence of these fumes for the worker's safety. When working with these metals, workers should be provided with a respirator for additional protection.

ELECTRICAL HAZARDS

Where oxy-acetylene torch welding uses a flame to raise the temperature of the metals, arc welding uses an electrical current. Thus, in addition to the flammability hazards associated with welding, **electrical hazards** must be addressed, as the welding units commonly run on 240 volts.

Arc welding should be prohibited in **wet environments**, including during or soon after a rain event. This will prevent the water from acting as a pathway for the current and shocking the welder. Additionally, insulating mats should be used if arc welding on a **metal surface** to reduce the risk of the welder becoming part of the electrical circuit. Welding lines and power cords must be **protected** from sparks and slag that can damage the insulation, which will eventually expose the wires. The unit should always be turned off or unplugged when not in use to prevent anyone from accidentally contacting the **leads**, which can result in a shock if still energized.

PHYSICAL HAZARDS

Welding uses high temperatures or high energy to melt and join two pieces of metal. The act of welding presents three main physical hazards to the welder.

- **Radiation**—the point of operation of the tip of the welding gun or torch emits light and energy that can damage the eye. The emitted light is very bright and can result in both acute and chronic eye injuries.
- **Burns**—the temperature required to melt the flux and join the metal is very high, which heats the surrounding metal to red-hot temperatures. The act of welding can also emit slag (molten metal) and sparks. All three conditions present a burn hazard to the welder.
- **Toxic fumes**—at the elevated temperatures involved in welding, certain metals can be vaporized and form inhalable fumes. Some metals, such as chromium VI and lead, are toxic to people, and controls must be implemented to protect the welder from negative health effects.

Hazards Associated with Cranes and Lifting Devices

CRANE OPERATIONS

Cranes have become vital tools to efficiently move or lift heavy materials. Cranes can reduce the number of trips required to relocate materials, move materials to elevated locations, and move heavy objects. However, the risks of using the equipment must be considered along with the benefits. Cranes that are **overloaded** can structurally fail or tip over, resulting in lost loads, injuries, or even fatalities. This accounts for over 80% of all crane accidents. The load can **fall** during movement because it exceeds the lifting capacity, the rigging is frayed, or the load is improperly secured. The jib, or "arm" of the crane, can come into contact with **overhead power lines**. If that happens, the crane becomes part of the circuit, creating the risk of shock or electrocution to the driver, those guiding the load with tethers, or even workers near the rig.

CRANE LOADS

A **crane** uses rigging, slings, wires, or ropes to attach a load to its hook. This results in a load that is suspended from the crane and can be subject to swinging, rotating, or otherwise moving in an unintended manner. This motion can **strike** workers, equipment, or buildings in the area, causing injury or damage. In high wind conditions, the load can cause damage similar to a wrecking ball. Additionally, if the rigging fails, the load can **fall** on people, materials, equipment, or other objects located in the fall zone. Rigging that is worn, insufficient for the load, damaged by heat or chemicals, or inappropriately attached to the load can result in a dropped load.

Hazards Associated with Rigging and Hoisting

HOISTING AND RIGGING

The terms "hoisting" and "rigging" are often used together when describing moving materials and loads. **Rigging** refers to the use of slings—ropes, wires, nets, or synthetic straps to **secure** the load to the lifting mechanism and prevent it from **falling**. The process of lifting the material and moving it is **hoisting**. The **hoist** may be a crane, a powered industrial truck, or other piece of equipment used to lift and move heavy items or bulk materials.

HAZARDS

The Occupational Safety and Health Administration identifies three main hazards associated with hoisting and rigging—fall hazards, struck-by hazards, and electrical hazards.

Fall hazards, which for hoisting means **dropped** loads, can be caused by failed or improper rigging. Wires, mesh, or straps can fail if worn, frayed, or placed on a sharp edge, resulting in a dropped load. Rigging that is not rated properly for the lift can snap or break due to being overloaded. **Uneven** work surfaces or **improperly balanced** loads can cause the hoist to tip over and fall. If the path of travel of the hoist is not cleared or contains uneven ground or changes in elevation such as unprotected holes, the hoist can topple over, spilling the load.

The load and the hoist can create **struck-by** hazards for nearby employees. Pedestrians that walk into the blind spots of the hoist can be struck by the hoist or the load. Loads that swing or twist out of control can pin a worker against nearby structures or equipment. If the hoist has a boom or other moving lifting mechanisms, these can create pinch points for worker body parts to get injured.

Overhead **electrical lines** can create hazards for any hoist or lifting operation. As the load or boom is lifted, overhead lines can contact the hoist, causing a shock to the equipment operator, those handling the load, or even those near the rig.

Hazards Associated with Electrical Work

VOLTAGE

Voltage is the potential difference between two parts of an electrical circuit. Whenever there is a difference of **potential** within a circuit, current will flow from the higher voltage point to the lower voltage point. The greater the difference, the greater the flow of electricity. In a circuit, the high-voltage point is either a power source or the negative terminal of a battery.

Construction standards will often have increased safety precautions when working with or near **high-voltage** lines and sources. The International Electrotechnical Commission (IEC) defines high-voltage as more than 1,500 volts for direct current (DC) or 1,000 volts for alternating current (AC).

ELECTRICAL CURRENT THRESHOLDS

The main driver behind damage to the body is the amount of electricity that enters the body, measured by the **current** in amperes (amps, A), and the **duration** of the exposure. The following lists the potential effects for a one (1) second exposure:

- 1 mA (milliamp): lowest **detection level**, can be perceived as a tingle
- 5 mA: lowest value that is considered harmless
- 10-20 mA: involuntary muscle contractions where someone may not be able to release the source of electricity, referred to as the **let go current**
- 30 mA: may cause temporary **respiratory paralysis** (exposures longer than 1 second can be fatal due to prolonged paralysis of the diaphragm)
- 100-300 mA: may cause **ventricular fibrillation** where exposures longer than 1 second can result in death

HAZARDS

Electricity and electrical equipment that is energized, improperly installed, or becomes damaged can introduce hazards in the workplace. Electrical circuits, wires, and equipment can **initiate fires** in the presence of flammable or combustible fuel sources. An act as simple as plugging equipment into a receptacle can create a spark that can act as a source of ignition. Frayed or damaged wires can arc, acting as an initiator for a fire.

Whenever a person contacts electricity, they can become **part of a circuit**, which can result in injury. This is typically referred to as a **shock**. Current easily flows through the body from where a person contacts the source to the ground. This can cause **burns** at the contact areas where electricity enters and leaves the body. Additionally, nerves use electrical impulses to control muscles. Therefore, exposure to electricity can cause **involuntary muscle contractions** and interfere with the motor nerves of the respiratory system and heart, potentially resulting in death.

VARIABLES WITHIN AN ELECTRIC CIRCUIT

An **electric circuit** can be described in terms of voltage, current, and resistance. **Resistance** is the impedance of electricity moving through the circuit—it slows down the movement of charge through the system. **Current** is the measure of how much electricity is moving through a specified part of the circuit. **Voltage** is the measure of the amount of work that can be done by the circuit, described as the pressure used to push electricity through the circuit.

Of those three variables, it is the current or the **amount** of electricity in the circuit that creates the risk for employees. If an employee becomes part of the circuit, the amount of electricity that flows through them can cause physiological responses, from a slight tingling sensation to burns to stopping the heart muscle. This interaction with current is referred to as a shock.

SHOCK VS. ELECTROCUTION

A person who comes into contact with electricity can become part of the **circuit**. Electricity flows through the path of least resistance, and a human, being composed of mostly salt water, provides a low resistance path to the earth. Exposure to electricity can result in a shock or electrocution. It must be noted that it is the amperage (current), not the voltage, that causes injury to the worker.

An electric **shock** is an exposure to electricity that does not result in death. Shocks include every exposure from the detection threshold of 0.2 mA to those that interrupt the heart rhythm at or around 75 mA. Additionally, electricity can cause burns at both the contact site and the site where the current leaves the body as well as damage internal organs. **Electrocution** is an electric shock that is fatal. Higher exposures (larger current) or longer exposures (unable to let go) can result in death by electrocution.

Hazards Associated with Excavations

EXCAVATION VS. TRENCH

An **excavation** is any man-made cut, trench, depression, hole, or pit dug into the earth. A **trench** is a specific type of excavation where one dimension is longer than the other. For trenches, the hole is narrower than it is long, and the depth is usually greater than the width. Trenches are created to either allow a worker to enter to perform installation or repair activities or to install items such as utility pipes or foundations.

PRINCIPAL HAZARD

The primary hazard associated with excavations is **cave-ins**. When soil is removed from an area, the surrounding soil must support additional weight it did not have to support before. As the excavation gets deeper, the weight of the soil at the top of the excavation no longer has lateral support, which can cause the belly to fail, trapping and potentially burying workers. The depth of the soil where excavation becomes a risk is dependent on the soil type, with sandy or loosely packed soils becoming unstable at shallower depths.

PHYSICAL HAZARDS

Since excavations are below grade, they create spaces with limited air flow. Toxic gases can collect in these spaces, which can create a **hazardous atmosphere** and displace oxygen. Toxic gases can come from combustion engines near the excavation, decomposing vegetation in the excavation, or damaged sewer lines in the excavation. If the excavation punctures a natural gas line, the excavation can fill with natural gas, creating a fire or explosion hazard as well as reduced oxygen levels that can suffocate entrants.

Due to the prevalence of **underground utilities**, there is a hazard of encountering buried electrical, water, sewer, or gas lines during digging. A backhoe or shovel can pierce electrical lines, resulting in shock or electrocution. Spiking underground water or sewer lines can cause the excavation to fill with water, trapping and potentially drowning workers.

ACTION LEVEL

OSHA has identified a depth of **five (5) feet** for an excavation where the risk of cave-ins increases dramatically. Because of this, OSHA requires that **controls** be implemented at or below this level to protect employees who must work in the excavations. As the hole deepens, the weight of the existing soil is now **unsupported** within the excavation and can fail, burying workers. The risk of cave-ins is dependent on **soil type** and excavation **depth**, but anything deeper than 5 feet must have a control implemented, such as benching, shoring, or sloping.

Hazards Associated with Office Environments

IMPROPER COMPUTER SETUP

The interaction between employees and their workstations is the foundation of the field of **ergonomics**. With more and more employees relying on computer workstations to conduct business, the proper setup of this equipment is critical to avoid long-term injuries. Often referred to as **musculoskeletal disorders (MSDs)**, injuries to tendons, ligaments, and muscles are associated with stagnant work positions such as **sitting** for extended periods of time, improper **workstation height**, reaching, and **repetitive motions**. These injuries are chronic, often realized after years of poor ergonomics, and may even require surgery to repair.

SLIP, TRIP, AND FALL HAZARDS

One of the primary culprits of office injuries is **slip, trip, and fall (STF)** hazards. STFs can result in cuts, bruises, fractures, and, in certain cases, fatalities. Office STF hazards include **wet floors**, caused by custodial activities, rain or snow, and spills that are not cleaned up quickly or properly. **Cords** for computers, projectors, and power can be improperly run across walkways or on paths of travel, resulting in a fall. **Rugs and carpets** that are not properly secured can also catch a person's foot, resulting in an injury.

EYESTRAIN

Eyestrain is defined as dryness, fatigue, or irritation of the eyes caused by intense use. In an office environment, **improper lighting** can result in eyestrain. Light that is too bright or too dim can negatively impact the eyes. Another common source of eyestrain is **computer** use. The glare from computer monitors, prolonged use of monitors, and improper positioning can cause the eyes to fatigue.

INDOOR AIR QUALITY

Indoor air quality (IAQ) refers to the air quality within an enclosed building and its effects on employees. IAQ includes impacts from chemicals, temperature, humidity, and biological materials.

Chemicals that can be breathed in by office workers include paint fumes, cleaning chemicals, and chemicals that are released from furnishings and decorations. The air **temperature** may be either too warm or too cold. In addition to employee comfort, excessive heat in humid environments can also contribute to biological growth.

Biological growth includes fungi, mold, and pollen from indoor plants that can cause short- or long-term health effects in employees. Employees may develop rashes, headaches, nausea, or even respiratory infections from poor indoor air quality. Long-term health effects can include respiratory diseases, heart disease, and, depending on the agent, cancer.

Hazards Associated with Motor Vehicle Operations

WORKPLACE FATALITIES

Accidents involving **motor vehicles** have historically been the leading cause of workplace fatalities. This includes accidents as the driver or the passenger and struck-by accidents of roadway workers. As many as 22% of workplace fatalities are a result of motor vehicle accidents. This includes truck drivers, public servants (such as police and fire personnel), and individuals who use passenger vehicles for work activities.

DRIVING LARGE TRUCKS

The Bureau of Labor Statistics defines a large truck as any vehicle having a gross weight in excess of 10,000 pounds. At this weight and at freeway speeds, large trucks do not handle in the same manner as passenger vehicles. Heavy vehicles require a significantly longer **stopping distance** to avoid collisions. The time and distance between brake pedal actuation and coming to a complete stop are much greater than for smaller vehicles. Vehicles of this size do not **handle** as well nor are they as responsive to driver controls. This makes avoiding roadway hazards more difficult. Additionally, the weight distribution makes heavy vehicles more prone to **tip over** during defensive driving maneuvers. Finally, heavy vehicles are more susceptible to bad weather due to their **high profile** (where the vehicle and trailer can act as a sail) and weight (increased stopping distance in rain and icy conditions).

DISTRACTED DRIVING

Distracted driving is the operation of a motor vehicle while performing any other activity that diverts attention from the driving task. When the driver's focus is not entirely on operating the vehicle, the risk for an **accident** increases significantly. Driver attention can be **diverted** by occupants, navigating unfamiliar territory, eating, drinking, other drivers, or mobile devices. Research has shown that drivers distracted by mobile devices can miss up to 50% of the information in the driving environment. In 2019, distracted driving contributed to 15% of all vehicle crashes in the United States, accounting for over 3,000 deaths.

Hazards Associated with Heavy Equipment Operations

HEAVY EQUIPMENT HAZARDS

Heavy equipment includes any large piece of mechanized equipment, such as excavators, loaders, backhoes, graders, or rollers. Due to the **size** and **design** of heavy equipment, its operators can be at risk of injury from the very equipment they are using.

The driver may have **limited visibility**, particularly when backing up, which can lead to the equipment running into structures or staged material which can fall onto the cab or result in the machine falling off ramps or roadways. Due to its weight and design, heavy equipment that is used on unstable or uneven ground can **tip over**, potentially injuring the driver. Equipment that digs can strike **buried utilities** which can cause an electric shock or puncture natural gas lines, creating a flammability hazard.

HAZARDS FOR NEARBY WORKERS

Heavy equipment machines, such as earth movers, backhoes, and graders, are large, powerful, and move massive loads, yet they have small fields of view relative to their size for the operators. Pedestrians near moving equipment can get **caught between** the equipment and other objects or have loads dropped on them, resulting in injury or even death. Due to its weight and design, heavy equipment that is used on unstable or uneven ground can **tip over**, potentially landing on those working near the machines. Finally, there is a potential for **operational failure** where the lifting mechanism or other operational piece fails, resulting in a dropped load or falling pieces of equipment.

LIMITED FIELD OF VIEW

Those who operate **heavy machinery** must be properly trained in the safe operation of the equipment. The cabin may be small in comparison to the vehicle, the cabin may not be centered, or the sheer size of the equipment may impact the operator's ability to see objects around the vehicle. This **impaired visibility** can increase the risk of the vehicle **striking** or otherwise running over a person working in the area. Areas behind the vehicle may have no direct line of vision for the driver, putting workers behind at risk of **struck-by** or **struck-between** accidents.

For the operator, the limited field may not provide a clear view of the roadway or path of travel. This can lead to a vehicle **tip-over** which can injure the driver. Also, lack of visibility above the vehicle can put the operator at risk of striking overhead powerlines, resulting in **shock or electrocution**.

Hazards Associated with Distractions While Working

DISTRACTED

Distracted can be defined as the inability to concentrate due to preoccupation with other concerns or information. Distracted can also be thought of as transferring the bulk of **thought processes** from a principal activity to another activity. For example, a person who is tightening a bolt can be distracted by a loud noise, a coworker asking a question, or their cell phone ringing, causing them to lose their grip on the wrench and drop the tool. If the worker is conducting a task that has risk such as welding or using a cutting tool, distraction can cause injuries such as burns or amputations.

LEADING CAUSE OF DISTRACTIONS

A 2020 study found that nearly 25% of industrial accidents were attributed to distractions caused by **mobile phones**. In the modern workplace, phones connect workers to information, supervisors, training content, and family. When a person is using their phone, their attention is divided between the device and their environment. This **divided attention** or distraction reduces their ability to input information from their surroundings, such as alarm signals, oncoming traffic, or a falling load. If a person is not focused on the risks of their environment due to the distraction caused by their device, they are at higher risk for injury at work.

CONTRIBUTION TO WORKPLACE INJURIES

Distraction can be described as losing **focus** on the primary task one is engaged in. Even in environments that appear to be risk-free such as offices, distraction can lead to injuries. An employee answering their phone while descending a staircase is no longer focused on where to place their foot and may fall, resulting in injury. Someone working on an assembly line who is tapped on the shoulder can leave their hand on the conveyor and get pulled into a pinch point. Distraction can also be caused by **hurrying** to finish a job, as the worker is more focused on the end product than the process. In these circumstances, distraction can lead to shortcutting machine guards, not following procedures, or putting limbs in harm's way to meet production or time goals. Any of those actions greatly increases the risk of injury.

Hazards Associated with Compressed Gas Storage and Use

GAS CYLINDERS

Compressed gas cylinders present both **physical** and **chemical** hazards to those who use them or work near them. Compressed gas cylinders can be pressurized as high as 2500 psi. At these pressures, damage to the valve assembly or cylinder body can result in an **uncontrolled release**. Leaking cylinders can become projectiles— even capable of penetrating walls. The release of high pressure near an employee can result in gas **penetrating** the skin and causing injury. The cylinders themselves are heavy enough that a falling cylinder can **fracture** a leg or foot or cause a **muscle strain** if an employee tries to catch it.

CONTENTS OF COMPRESSED GAS CYLINDERS

Compressed gas cylinders are used to store a variety of materials, including inert, toxic, corrosive, and flammable chemicals. Damaged cylinders or improperly secured connections can result in **leaks** that expose employees to **toxic gases** and their associated health effects. Even gases that present no health hazards, such as inert gases, can displace oxygen in an enclosed space. As the concentration of gas increases, the **oxygen level** in a space can become dangerously low, which can impact employees and, in extreme cases, result in death. Fuel gas cylinders present a **flammability hazard** and must be protected from ignition sources to prevent fires and explosions. **Corrosive** gases can irritate the skin, eyes, and mucous membranes of those working in the area and can damage nearby equipment and materials.

CAUSES OF GAS LEAKS

Cylinders may contain asphyxiants, corrosives, flammables, or toxic gases. Any leak can lead to an exposure, increased fire risk, and loss of material. Gas leaks can be caused by minute **holes** due to oxidation (rust) in the steel shell caused by water, contact with bare soil, or the presence of other corrosive chemicals. Improperly seated **regulators** can lead to gas leaks if the threads are not properly aligned and the junction not appropriately tightened. **Excessive heat** applied to the cylinder can cause over-pressurization, which may exceed the ability of the regulator or valve to safely contain the gas. **Dirt** on seals, gaskets, or valves can impact proper seating of regulators and allow gas to leak out of the system.

Hazard Controls

The Hierarchy of Controls

HAZARD CONTROL HIERARCHY

The **National Institute of Safety and Health (NIOSH)** has developed a **hierarchy of controls** as a recommended approach to mitigating any hazard. The hierarchy establishes the order of strategies to be used to address hazards based on their effectiveness. Hazard controls should be assessed in the following order: **1) elimination, 2) substitution, 3) engineering controls, 4) administrative controls,** and **5) personal protective equipment.**

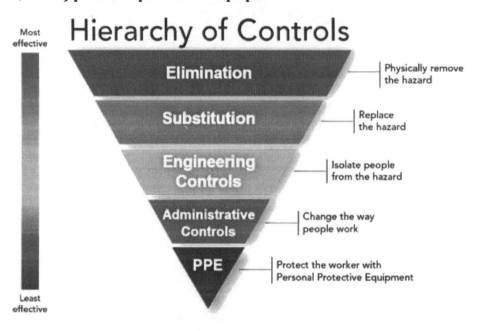

Hierarchy of Controls

Most effective → Least effective		
Elimination	Physically remove the hazard
Substitution	Replace the hazard
Engineering Controls	Isolate people from the hazard
Administrative Controls	Change the way people work
PPE	Protect the worker with Personal Protective Equipment

> **Review Video: Risk Management and Hazard Control**
> Visit mometrix.com/academy and enter code: 625808

Per the hierarchy, the preferred method is to remove or **eliminate** the hazard from the workplace. If there is no hazard, there is no chance of harm. If removal is not possible, then the next method is to evaluate **replacing** the hazardous task with one that is less hazardous. For example, using water-based chemicals removes the flammability hazard associated with solvent-based materials. If replacement is not feasible, then engineering controls should be evaluated. **Engineering controls** are designed to remove or divert the hazard from the worker at the source. For example, ventilation systems can be used to remove combustible dusts from a manufacturing process. If an engineering control is not feasible, then an administrative control should be examined for its effectiveness. **Administrative controls** include policies and procedures to reduce exposures, such as Standard

Operating Procedures and warning signs. If no other control is feasible or while other controls are being implemented, **personal protective equipment** (gloves, respirators, and protective clothing) can be used to reduce potential exposure to the hazard.

PRIORITIZING ENGINEERING CONTROLS

The benefit of an **engineering control** is that it functions **independently** of the worker. The control does not require intervention or activation by the individual who may be near the hazard. Also, the functionality and effectiveness of the control are not dependent on who is near the hazard—the level of protection is always maintained for all employees. For example, if there is a guard shielding the rollers of a conveyor belt, then the pinch point hazard they present is adequately controlled. The worker who is inspecting finished product on the line does not have to take any action to be protected, and every inspector on the line receives the same level of protection.

RELYING SOLELY ON ADMINISTRATIVE HAZARD CONTROLS

Administrative controls are **policies** and **procedures**, including **signage**, that are used to reduce the employee's exposure to the hazard. These types of controls do not impact the magnitude of the hazard but function more by reducing the **proximity** of the employee to the risk or decreasing the **duration** of exposure. For example, a policy that prohibits workers from wearing gloves near moving machinery parts is designed to prevent pinch point injuries if the glove gets caught. However, the effectiveness of administrative controls is dependent on the worker recognizing the hazard and following the procedure by not wearing gloves. If a posted sign requires hearing protection, the employee must see the sign, recognize the hazard, and obtain the hearing protection. Otherwise, the control is not effective.

PERSONAL PROTECTIVE EQUIPMENT

On the **hierarchy of hazard controls**, personal protective equipment (PPE) is considered the least effective method of controlling a hazard. The reasons PPE is the least preferred method include its reliance on:

- Proper **selection**—PPE is only effective if it protects against the known or suspected hazard. For example, using leather gloves while working with corrosive chemicals will not protect hands from irritation or burns.
- Proper **sizing**—a petite person who is wearing an extra-large respirator will not get a proper seal, thereby rendering the PPE useless. Also, improperly sized equipment, either too small or too large, can introduce additional hazards such as tripping over safety shoes that are too big or a loss of sensation in the fingers when gloves are too small.
- Proper **donning**—if PPE is not put on ("donned") correctly, its effectiveness is not maximized. Foam earplugs that are not placed into the ear canal will not shield the wearer from hazardous noise.

- Proper **maintenance**—PPE that is worn or damaged will not provide the intended level of protection. A fall protection harness with a frayed strap could fail to stop a falling worker.

Controls Associated with Safety Systems/Interlocks

SAFETY INTERLOCK

A safety **interlock** is a protective device installed on a piece of equipment that prevents a worker from being exposed to a hazard while the machine is operating. An interlock device may either be a **safety switch** or a **locking device**. The interlock may either prevent operation or startup when it is interrupted.

Safety interlock switches are connected to the power source. If the **contact** is interrupted, such as when a protective shield is opened, the power to the equipment is shut off to put the machine into a safe state. Interlock locking devices will not allow a guard to be opened or removed while the machine is running—power must be off before the **lock** will release, allowing access to the hazardous area.

CLASSES OF SAFETY INTERLOCKS

A **safety interlock** is a device that prevents a person from being exposed to an equipment hazard. The device will either **interrupt** the power, shutting the machine down, or will not allow a guard to be **moved** until the machine is in a safe state. There are two broad classes of interlocks—mechanical and non-mechanical.

Mechanical interlocks have a physical component that prevents the operation of the machine, such as a pin, latch, or lock. There is **physical contact** between the interlock and the system, meaning it must be physically removed or engaged, either manually or automatically, for the system to be rendered safe.

Non-mechanical interlocks include such items as electromagnets and optics. If an electromagnet is interrupted, the circuit is disrupted and the safety system will be activated, such as by cutting power to the equipment. Optical systems, such as beams or light curtains, sense an interruption in the light path, which then engages the safety system or disengages the operation of the equipment.

EFFECTIVE SAFETY INTERLOCK SYSTEM

Safety interlocks prevent a worker from being exposed to a machine hazard by either **isolating** the power when the interlock is open or **preventing access** to the hazard while the machine is operating. Guards are critical in preventing worker injuries caused by blades, pinch points, and moving parts.

In order to be effective, the interlock system must be **reliable** and **secure**. An interlock system that doesn't function when needed is not effective and will not consistently prevent injuries. The interlock must function properly every time it is needed and should not fail to activate. In addition to being reliable, the interlock must not be able to be defeated. If an interlock can be bypassed, short-circuited, or is otherwise not secure, it will not keep workers safe.

INTERLOCKS NEAR ROBOTS

Industrial robots are used to perform work that is difficult for humans to perform, dangerous for workers, or at rates of speed that exceed human capabilities. However, these machines still require human interaction, such as for maintenance, repair, or calibration. As the robot is programmed to execute functions within its working area, termed an "**envelope**," safety interlocks must be installed on the **gates** surrounding the robot's work area. The interlock will **shut down** the robot's operation so the entrant is not struck by the arm, pinned between the arm and the workpiece, or harmed by the operations being conducted by the mechanical system.

Controls Associated with Chronic Health Hazards

CHRONIC

A **chronic exposure** to a hazard is one that occurs over a **long** period of time and is typically associated with a **small amount** of stressor at any one time. A common example is lung cancer caused by cigarette smoking—the amount of harmful chemical exposure from a single cigarette is relatively small, but a lifetime exposure will have harmful effects. The health effects of a chronic exposure may not be readily identifiable and may not be realized until a period of time after the exposure; these are termed "latent" health effects. In the example of cigarette smoking, lung cancer or chronic obstructive pulmonary disease (COPD) will not be detected for many years and can be fatal. Workers may experience a chronic exposure to chemicals, radiation, noise, metal fumes, or other materials based on their occupation and work environment.

CHEMICAL EXPOSURE
USING HIERARCHY OF CONTROLS TO CONTROL CHRONIC EXPOSURE

Long-term exposure to health hazards can result in **irreversible** medical conditions. However, an employer can leverage the hierarchy of hazard controls to reduce the risk associated with chronic exposures. As an example, some chemical wax strippers use solvents or corrosive chemicals to remove the old wax. Over their career, custodial staff could develop respiratory symptoms or skin sensitivity from this constant, low-dose exposure.

The employer can **eliminate** the hazard from the work environment by either contracting out the wax work or switching to a physical system in lieu of the chemical stripper. Either choice will remove the chemical exposure hazard from their staff. If that is not feasible, the employer could evaluate low-VOC products to reduce the amount of volatile chemicals the staff are exposed to—**substituting** a less hazardous floor stripper. A potential **engineering control** is to use fans to push the vapors out of the work area, thereby reducing employee exposure. Establishing a schedule for treating floors once a year is an **administrative control** to reduce the frequency of the custodians stripping the floors and the resulting exposure. As a last choice, the employer could create a respiratory protection program and require the use of personal protective equipment (a respirator and chemical-resistant gloves) whenever wax stripping is conducted.

ROUTES OF ENTRY

An individual can be exposed to a chemical hazard by one of the four **routes of entry**—injection, ingestion, absorption, and inhalation.

- **Injection** is the subcutaneous exposure of a chemical which allows it to bypass the protective layer of the skin. An example of an injection exposure would be a broken chemical container that pierces the skin, allowing the chemical to enter the bloodstream.
- **Ingestion** is exposure to a chemical by mouth, which causes an exposure by way of the digestive system. A person who has touched a hazardous material and then eats, drinks, applies cosmetics, takes medication, or smokes can transfer the material from their hands into their mouth, resulting in an exposure.
- **Absorption** is the movement of a chemical through the intact skin. Skin absorption can occur when certain chemicals are spilled or splashed on unprotected flesh. As the concentration of the chemical is higher on the surface of the skin then it is on the inside of the body, the chemical will move to the area of lower concentration—a process called diffusion.
- **Inhalation** is the most common route of entry for hazardous materials. High concentrations of water-soluble chemicals can overwhelm the protection of the **upper respiratory system** and enter the lungs. Chemicals that are not water-soluble can bypass the protective mucosa in the upper respiratory system and pass into the lungs. Once in the lungs, chemicals can damage the lung tissue or pass into the blood through the **alveoli**, where they can negatively impact the body.

REDUCING EXPOSURE TO A RESPIRABLE HAZARDOUS MATERIAL

In order for a chemical to be **inhaled**, it must be airborne. Once it is airborne, it can be inhaled by an employee and get into the respiratory system, where it can cause damage. Thus, if the chemical can be prevented from entering the lungs, the chance of a chemical-related injury or illness is reduced. The risk of an inhalation hazard can be reduced by substituting with a less volatile substance, ventilation, or respiratory protection.

Chemicals that are **volatile** (airborne at or near ambient temperatures) are easily inhaled. These chemicals are usually detected by their odor. Thus, if there are formulations that are less volatile, such as water-based instead of oil-based, then the risk of inhalation is decreased. If there is not an adequate substitute, then **ventilation** can be used to increase the amount of fresh air or remove the airborne contaminant. General ventilation can keep fresh air blowing toward workers, reducing the amount of chemical they are exposed to. **Local exhaust ventilation** can be used to remove chemical vapors before they are inhaled by workers. Vapors are pulled into an exhaust hose and ejected away from the work area. If ventilation cannot be used, then employees can use **respiratory protection**.

PROTECTING WORKERS FROM CHRONIC HEALTH HAZARDS

A **chronic health hazard** results from an **extended exposure** to a physical or chemical hazard. The negative health effects typically arise well after the exposure. In order to protect workers from long-term health risks, employers can reduce the employee's exposure and use medical monitoring.

Exposure is defined as the amount of time an employee is exposed to a hazard and the magnitude of the hazard—how long and how much. Thus, either the amount of **time** or the **magnitude** can be reduced to lower the health risk. For example, job rotation can be used to reduce the amount of time the employee is exposed— janitorial crews can be rotated between using chemical strippers and removing trash. The magnitude of the hazard can be reduced by hazard controls, such as using personal protective equipment.

Employees can also be subject to **medical monitoring** for certain health hazards. Employees working with lead can be subject to periodic blood tests to determine their exposure. If lead is detected in an employee's blood and it reaches a certain level, measures can be taken to both reduce the employee's exposure and treat the medical condition before it becomes irreversible.

Controls Associated with Acute Health Hazards

ACUTE

Exposure to chemicals can be described as acute or chronic. An **acute** exposure is typically a large amount of chemical coming into contact with the body over a short period of time. Such an exposure would occur when a painter drops a can of thinner and the lid comes off, splashing all over them. Health effects from an acute exposure are typically **immediately** realized and tend to resolve quickly—the painter may develop a rash that disappears after a few days. However, if the exposure is to a toxic or highly toxic material, the acute exposure could result in death.

PREVENTING CHEMICAL EXPOSURES BY INJECTION

In order for an employee to have an **injection exposure**, the chemical must have a means to pierce or otherwise enter the skin. When sharp objects coated or contaminated with chemicals are stepped on or puncture an arm, an injection injury will result. High-pressure gas lines where the line pressure exceeds 100 psi also present injection hazards by piercing the skin, allowing the gas to enter the body.

Injection hazards can be controlled by **cleaning** up spills immediately and, by way of proper **housekeeping**, removing or otherwise managing sharp objects. Steel-shank boots can prevent puncture wounds to the feet. Using **regulators** and reducing line pressures can prevent gas injection injuries.

PREVENTING CHEMICAL EXPOSURES BY INGESTION

The primary mode of getting exposed to a chemical by **ingestion** is when the employee has hand-to-mouth contact with contaminated hands. Less frequently, ingestion exposures occur when an employee is exposed to a large amount of chemical to the face that enters an open mouth and is subsequently swallowed.

The most effective control for ingestion exposures is for employees to use **protective gloves** when handling chemicals and remove those gloves before eating, drinking, smoking, applying cosmetics, or taking medications. An employee should always wash their hands after handling hazardous materials, even if gloves were worn, and before they take a rest break. Chemical exposures to the mouth can also be prevented by using face shields that protect the entire face.

PREVENTING CHEMICAL EXPOSURES BY ABSORPTION

An absorption exposure is when an employee is exposed to a chemical that, by its nature, can migrate through intact skin and enter the bloodstream. In order to prevent **absorption** exposures to hazardous chemicals, employers can use one of three methods—elimination, substitution, or personal protective equipment. As with any other occupational hazard, the best control method is to **remove** the hazard completely. The job requiring the material should be assessed to determine whether it is necessary for the project. If the process is required, then the next best choice is to determine whether there is a **less hazardous** (non-skin-absorbing) formulation that provides an equivalent product. If the process cannot be eliminated and the chemical cannot be exchanged, then the last method to avoid skin exposure is to use **personal protective equipment (PPE).** Skin-absorbing chemicals will require the use of impermeable chemical suits that prevent the chemical from coming into contact with the skin.

Controls Associated with Working at Heights

FALL PROTECTION CONTROL MEASURES

In general industry, meaning not during construction, shipbuilding, marine, or mining activities, an employer is required to implement **fall protection** controls when employees will be working at any elevation where they will be exposed to an unprotected side that is **four (4) feet or more** above the next level. For example, employees who work in or around loading docks that are more than 4 feet deep must be protected from falling into the vehicle bay. In industrial settings, employees who will be on observation platforms or catwalks more than 4 feet above machinery must be protected from falls.

PERSONAL FALL PREVENTION CONTROLS

There are three general types of fall prevention controls that can be used when fall protection is required: fall arrest systems, guardrails, and safety nets. **Fall arrest systems,** as described in 29 CFR 1910.140, consist of an anchor point, a lanyard, a deceleration device, and a body harness. They are designed to decelerate an already falling worker to reduce the risk or degree of injury caused by a fall. **Guardrails** are temporary or permanent structures installed at or near an unprotected edge to prevent a fall. Guardrail systems use posts, a top rail, and midrails to keep workers from falling. A **safety net** is a system installed at or below an exposed edge to catch a falling worker or large items of debris. The net does not prevent falls but catches a worker who has already fallen, preventing injury. The requirements for both systems are described in 29 CFR 1910.29.

PREVENTING INJURIES FROM FALLING OBJECTS

Objects that fall from one level to another can cause major injuries when they strike someone working or walking below and can even result in death. The risk of **objects falling** from heights and striking workers below can be reduced by the installation of toeboards, the use of canopies, or by deploying barricades.

A **toeboard** is a raised barrier that is installed at or near the unprotected edge to prevent objects from getting pushed, kicked, or otherwise falling off the edge. An employer may opt to erect **canopies** to prevent falling objects from hitting those walking or working on a lower level. The canopy provides a protective "roof" so that any debris is caught or deflected by the canopy. Another option is for the employer to establish **fall zones** by using barricades or fencing to keep employees out of the area where falling objects from upper levels may land. This provides a designated area where materials can be thrown or dropped from higher levels.

FALL RESTRAINT VS. FALL ARREST SYSTEMS

The risk of injuries caused by falls can be reduced by fall restraint or fall arrest systems. A **fall restraint** system prevents a fall from happening. Lifelines and guardrails are both examples of fall restraint systems. A **fall arrest** system is designed to **slow or stop** a falling worker to prevent injury or reduce the severity of the injury by absorbing some of the energy related to the fall. Fall arrest systems include safety nets and personal fall arrest systems, which consist of an anchor point, tether, deceleration device, and body harness. Fall restraint systems prevent the fall from happening, while fall arrest systems slow a fall that has already happened.

GUARDRAILS

Guardrails are **fall restraint** systems that are installed on or near unprotected edges to prevent workers from falling and getting injured. Per 29 CFR 1910.29, guardrails must:

- Have a **top rail** that is 39 to 45 inches from the surface on which they are installed, and the top rail must be at least one-quarter (1/4) inch in diameter
- Have a midrail, screen, mesh, or other **intermediate structural member** if there is no parapet or wall that is at least 21 inches high
- Be able to withstand an outward or downward **force** of at least 200 pounds
- Be **smooth** or otherwise free of presenting cut or puncture hazards to employees or having the potential to snag clothes
- Not have top rails or midrails that **overhang** the terminal post of the guardrail system

- When used for access points such as ladders, be outfitted with a gate or be offset from one another to prevent workers from accidentally walking and falling into the ladderway

PERSONAL FALL ARREST SYSTEMS

Personal fall arrest systems (PFAS) are a type of personal protective equipment that is designed to **decelerate** a fall to reduce the energy and stop a fall before the worker strikes the next level. PFAS consist of a **body harness** (body belts are prohibited), **connector**, **lanyard**, and **anchor**. Connectors, where the lanyard is attached to the harness, shall be made of drop forged steel, corrosion-resistant, and rated for 5,000 pounds. Snap hooks cannot be attached to webbing, another snap hook, a lifeline, or to a d-ring that another snap hook is attached to. Lifelines and lanyards shall be constructed of synthetic materials and have a maximum **free-fall distance** of 2 feet before they deploy or self-retract. Anchors must be able to withstand **5,000 pounds per worker** attached to the anchorage and may not be used for any other anchorage while an employee is attached. Harnesses must have connection points in the middle of the back and be **inspected** before each use, and employees must be **trained** on proper inspection and donning of the harness.

POSITIONING DEVICES

A **positioning device**, as described in 29 CFR 1910.140, is a fall protection device that allows a worker to be suspended along a **vertical** surface and perform work. It consists of a **body belt or harness** that is specially rigged to keep both hands free. It must be noted that this is one of the few allowances for the use of a body belt as a fall protection device. The system allows a worker to use both hands while suspended along the working surface. Workers on elevated poles can use a positioning device to allow them to repair or install lines or other equipment.

Controls Associated with Excavations

REDUCING THE RISK OF CAVE-IN

The highest risk for employees working in excavations is becoming trapped during a **cave-in** where the sides fail. Failure of an excavation typically starts at the bottom of the sides, where the supported weight is greatest. In order to keep the sides of an excavation from failing, an employer may use one of three techniques: shoring, sloping, or benching.

Shoring is the installation of a **physical system** to keep the sides from caving in. Shoring includes systems of wood or metal or may be a prefabricated trench box that is lowered into the excavation. These systems provide a safe space for workers and stabilize the sides of the excavation.

Sloping and **benching** are techniques to reduce the amount of soil weight on unsupported sides of an excavation. In sloping, the sides of the excavation are gradually **cut back** from the floor, resulting in a shape that resembles a ramp. In benching, the sides of the excavation are "**stair-stepped**" toward the top so that any one "step" is not supporting the entire mass of soil. These two techniques require more space at the dig location to achieve the optimal angle for preventing a cave-in.

REDUCING THE RISK OF STRIKING UNDERGROUND UTILITIES

Underground utilities, including water, electrical, gas, data, and sewer, can be hazardous if they are contacted during an excavation. Excavations can be flooded by water or sewage, they can fill with toxic and flammable gases, or the equipment operator can receive a shock from an electrical line. Prior to digging, utility companies can be contacted to **survey** the scene and **identify** the location of their respective services. Alternatively, third-party **vendors** can be hired to locate buried utilities and identify safe areas for digging.

BENCHING VS. SLOPING

Benching and **sloping** are two techniques that can be used to prevent cave-ins in an excavation. Both techniques rely on removing soil at an **angle** where the top of the excavation is larger than the bottom to relieve the weight of the soil on the walls of the hole.

In benching, the angle is created by a series of **steps**. Each step has a vertical or near-vertical face and a horizontal top so that the excavation walls resemble a bleacher or staircase. The Occupational Safety and Health Administration (OSHA) allows step heights up to five (5) feet; however, the first step is limited to a maximum height of four (4) feet.

In **sloping**, the sides of the excavation are sloped away from the bottom of the hole. Where benching results in a series of steps, sloped excavations resemble ramps that descend into the hole.

SHORING

Where sloping and benching remove additional soil to prevent cave-ins, **shoring** uses a **physical support** to reduce the hazard. By using a combination of plates and supports, a physical **barrier** is inserted into the excavation to prevent a cave-in and support the sides of the hole. Shoring can be used when the depth of the excavation makes benching or sloping impractical, such as excavations in a street. A shoring system consists of **posts, wales, struts,** and **sheeting** and can be made of timber or metal. Metal systems can be either **hydraulic** or **pneumatic**. In both systems, the hydraulic or pneumatically operated beams are pumped against the walls like pistons, where they apply pressure to prevent cave-ins.

SHORING SYSTEM

A shoring system consists of posts, wales, struts, and sheeting to hold back the walls of an excavation. **Sheeting** is the material that contacts the soil, creating the wall of the shoring system. The sheeting keeps the soil in place and is supported by the other shoring members. **Wales** are the horizontal members that run along the sheeting, providing supports for the sheeting and an anchor point for struts. The wales distribute the pressure of the struts to counter the weight of the soil against the sheeting. **Struts** are cross-braces that support both sides of the system and push against the soil. **Posts** are vertical elements that support the wales and the sheeting.

TRENCH SHIELD

Where a shoring system is the insertion of timber or metal to support soil and prevent a cave-in for any excavation, a shield system is designed to protect workers in the hole. **Shield systems**, such as trench boxes, are inserted into the excavation, and soil is **backfilled** between the shield and the wall to stabilize the shield. The excavation should be planned such that the spacing between the soil and the shield, which will require backfilling, is minimized. Shield systems can be used in conjunction with sloping or benching.

Shield systems can have an **economic advantage**, as they can be rented for less than it would cost to install a shoring system at the site. The metal boxes are **stronger** than timber structures and have fewer cross-bracing elements, which allows for easier movement and lowering of materials into the excavation. Finally, when a trench shield is used, **additional excavation** is allowed to occur below the walls of the shield, to a maximum unprotected depth of two (2) feet below the shield, if conditions allow. In a sloping or benching system, additional excavation would be necessary to account for the additional depth. In a shoring system, additional members would have to be installed to reduce the risk of cave-in.

ANGLE OF REPOSE

Angle of repose is the natural angle that a pile of a particular type of soil or gravel will attain when it is piled. The angle depends on the constituents of the soil, meaning that sand, clay, and aggregate will have different final angles. If a pile of soil is made steeper than the angle of repose, the pile is subject to **collapsing**. This limitation must be taken into consideration when identifying a location for the spoils pile near an excavation—if the removed soil is piled greater than the angle of repose and is too close to the hole, the soil could collapse into the hole, trapping workers.

Controls Associated with Industrial Lifting Vehicles

REDUCING THE RISK TO PEDESTRIANS

Forklifts are present in many warehouse and manufacturing environments where heavy loads must be moved and lifted. These areas may also contain other workers, moving among and between workstations. Thus, control measures must be implemented to reduce the risk of a pedestrian being struck by a forklift.

The hazard can be eliminated by **prohibiting** pedestrians from being in the area where forklifts are active. If keeping people out of the area is not feasible, then designated pedestrian **pathways** can be marked on the floor. Another administrative control is to install **visual indicators**, such as lights, or use **audible indicators**, such as horns or warning devices, attached to the vehicles to notify pedestrians of an approaching forklift.

PREVENTING LOADS FROM FALLING OFF

The most commonly identified cause of dropped loads from industrial lift vehicles is **overloading**. Thus, the maximum load rating of the vehicle should be clearly **marked** on the equipment, and the **weight** of all loads to be handled should be clearly visible. This will allow the operator to determine whether the vehicle can and should attempt the lift. Loads should be prepared in such a way that they are **properly balanced** on the lifting mechanism. Off-balance loads increase the risk of both losing the load and the lift vehicle tipping over. Finally, **speed limits** for the vehicles should be established and enforced to prevent dropping loads during cornering and traveling on ramps.

TRAINING PROGRAM

Overloading, improper loading, and improper use of forklifts and other industrial lifting vehicles are the primary causes of incidents involving these vehicles. Forklift incidents can result in injuries to both operators and pedestrians as well as the financial loss of the dropped load. Therefore, OSHA has put an emphasis on **driver training** to reduce the risk of injuries, incidents, and lost materials during lifting operations. As outlined in 29 CFR 1910.178, operators must be trained on:

- Operating instructions, warnings, and precautions
- The difference between a lift and a car
- Location, function, and use of all controls
- How the engine works
- Steering and handling of the vehicle
- Visibility, capacity, and stability
- Inspection, maintenance, and proper operation of the vehicle

Training programs must include both a classroom portion and a practical **demonstration** of ability before an individual is authorized to operate a lifting vehicle.

AVOIDING LOADS FALLING DURING A HOISTING OPERATION

Loads falling during a lift can have fatal impacts on workers. Falling loads can be caused by overloading, defective components, or equipment failure.

Overloading during a lift is typically attributed to a lack of training for the rigger on how to correct for the working load limit (WLL) of the lift. The WLL corrects the stated load capacity of a **sling** to the configuration being used for the actual lift. Angled slings must be adjusted down for the tension factor, while multiple vertical slings increase the load capacity.

Aged, damaged, or otherwise compromised slings and hooks can **fail**, resulting in a dropped load. Pre-shift **inspections** of all slings, straps, chains, and wire ropes should be conducted to evaluate their integrity before use. Slings should be labeled with their capacity, free from any splits, tears, or rips, and, for synthetic slings, protected from being cut by sharp edges during the lift. Wire ropes should be inspected before each shift for broken wires, bird-nesting, or other indications of

71

potential failure. Hooks and latches should be inspected for jaw spread and cracks that would necessitate their replacement.

OSHA also outlines specific hoisting **equipment inspections** that must occur to make sure the boom, drums, reeves, or other equipment does not fail during the lift. Cranes must be inspected after assembly (if erected on-site), before each shift, monthly, and annually.

OUTRIGGERS

An **outrigger** is a deployable stabilizer that is found on mobile cranes. The outriggers provide a **stable base** for the crane and, when properly deployed, reduce the chance of tipping. Outriggers achieve this increased stability by **distributing** the weight of the load over a wider area. Some outriggers allow for partial deployment, which allows them to be used on uneven ground, per the manufacturer's stability charts. Outriggers should be outfitted with **pads** to prevent the feet from sinking into soft or unstable ground. When present on a mobile crane, employees must be **trained** to properly deploy the outriggers for every lift.

PRECAUTIONS NEAR ENERGIZED POWER LINES

Contacting an energized transmission line can cause **electric shock** to the crane operator and those near the crane or assisting with the load. To eliminate the electrical hazard, the lines can be **de-energized** and **grounded**. If the lines cannot be de-energized, the employer can ensure that the crane maintains the required **minimum safe distance** based on the voltage of the line (20 feet for less than 350,000 volts, 50 feet if the line voltage is between 350,000 and 1,000,000 volts, consult an engineer for more than 1,000,000 volts). If a minimum safe distance will be used instead of de-energizing, a pre-project meeting must occur to review the location of the lines, and the lift must use a spotter, proximity warning device, or other visible indicator to warn the operator they are nearing the safe working limit.

Instead of a minimum safe distance, the employer may determine the **specific distance** based on the exact voltage. This distance is determined using a table located in the OSHA construction standard.

SIGNAL PERSON

A **signal person** acts as the eyes of a crane operator and is external to the crane itself. They position themselves in a safe area away from the load but in a position where they can **see** the direction of travel of the load or the crane. A signal person is **required** whenever the load must travel or be placed in an area the operator **cannot** see, when the equipment is **moving** and the path is obscured, near **electrical lines**, or whenever a signal person will increase the **safety** of the operation. The person must be **trained** in standard hand signal methodology, have a basic understanding of how the crane works as well as its limitations, and pass a test to demonstrate their understanding.

Controls Associated with Motor Vehicle Operations

DEFENSIVE DRIVING COURSE

With motor vehicle accidents being one of the major causes of employee injuries as well as fiscal loss for companies, teaching employees how to safely operate vehicles will reduce the risk of accidents. With nearly 90% of all accidents being caused by errors by one or both drivers, the Department of Transportation recommends **defensive driving** training to reduce the number of accidents on the roadways. Reinforcing proper following distances, following the speed limit, obeying all laws, and staying focused on the driving task are some of the techniques that can reduce the risk to employees who drive on company business.

PREVENTING DISTRACTED DRIVING

According to the American Safety Council, **distracted driving** is a contributing factor in hundreds of thousands of vehicle accidents each year. In modern society, the primary culprit is the mobile phone. Employers can reduce the risk by creating and enforcing a **zero tolerance policy** for cell phone use while driving.

Employers must **inform** employees of the hazards of driving while texting or talking, in that these activities remove attention from the road and associated hazards. Employers should supplement such a policy with an **understanding** that employees who are driving will not be able to answer calls immediately. Certain occupations, such as sales and customer service, may have to adjust the expectations of both supervisors and customers in an effort to prioritize the safety of those who drive as part of their work. Contrary to expected results, 19% of the Fortune 500 companies who instituted a no-answer policy saw an increase in productivity, versus 7% who saw a decrease.

INSPECTION REQUIREMENTS FOR COMMERCIAL VEHICLES

The Department of Transportation, under 49 CFR 396.17, requires that any vehicle that has a gross weight of at least 10,001 pounds or any size vehicle that transports hazardous materials must undergo a periodic **inspection**. This inspection must occur at least once **every 12 months**.

The inspection is comprehensive to ensure that the vehicle is fit for travel, is mechanically sound, and that all safety systems are functioning correctly. The inspection must address the brakes, couplers, exhaust system, fuel system, lights, steering, suspension, frame, wheels, tires, and windshield.

PREVENTING VEHICLE ACCIDENTS ATTRIBUTED TO FATIGUE

Fatigue can be described as physical or mental exertion that has resulted in impaired performance. The brain or body has been taxed to the point that it is not functioning at peak performance. The driving task requires **mental focus** to process multiple streams of information as well as **physical ability** to control the vehicle. Fatigue can be caused by lack of sleep, strenuous physical or mental work, stress, and substances such as drugs and alcohol.

The impact of fatigue can be mitigated using a variety of strategies. Drivers are less likely to be drowsy during the day, meaning night driving should be restricted. Employees should be encouraged to **self-assess** their mental and physical state to make sure they are alert before getting behind the wheel. Policies prohibiting the use of drugs or alcohol while driving on company business will also reduce the risk of accidents.

Controls Associated with Heavy Equipment Operations

PROTECTIVE MEASURES

Due to the size of the equipment and the limited visibility of the operator, especially while backing up, heavy equipment can pose a hazard to nearby workers. Workers can be struck by the vehicle, the load, or other movable parts, such as extension arms, buckets, or graders. Employees who will be working near or passing by heavy equipment should be issued **high-visibility clothing**, so they stand out from the environment and catch the eye of the operator. Vehicles should only reverse if the driver has a clear view of what is behind them, such as by using a spotter or backup camera. Heavy equipment should be used with audible or visual **reverse indicators** to warn when the vehicle will be moving. Equipment should have **functioning headlights, taillights,** and **brake lights** to increase its visibility to pedestrians as well as assist in indicating its direction of travel. Employees should be **trained** on precautions that are necessary when working or walking near heavy equipment.

PROTECTING DRIVERS

Whenever heavy equipment is being used, the employer should make sure that all roadways are **adequate** for travel to prevent tipping. Roads and ramps should be durable, stable, and large enough for the equipment. Heavy equipment shall be outfitted with a **Roll-Over Protection System (ROPS)** to provide the driver additional protections in the event of a tip-over. Vehicles that are top loaded (such as dump trucks) shall have **canopies or cab shields** to protect the driver from material that may fall and strike the cab while being loaded. All vehicles shall have **seat belts**, and their use should be required while the vehicle is in motion. All drivers shall be **trained** on load limits, proper loading, safe operation, pre-shift inspections, use of controls, warning systems, and all safety features for the equipment they will be using.

SPOTTERS

A **spotter** is a designated individual in constant communication with the operator of heavy equipment, to reduce the risk of accidents involving the equipment. Heavy equipment has significantly large **blind spots** where the operator is unable to see people and objects in the vicinity. The spotter works with the operator to navigate safely through the environment to avoid other workers and objects and remain on the proper pathway. The spotter should be in constant **visual communication** using hand signals or direct communication via radio with the operator. Spotters can also communicate with workers in the area to provide clear space for the equipment while it is moving or operating. Spotters should wear **high-visibility**

clothing so they are clearly visible against the background and be trained in a hand signal communication system.

WORKING AROUND OVERHEAD POWERLINES

Whenever there are overhead powerlines present and heavy equipment will be used, **signs** should be installed to indicate the presence of the lines. When equipment is moving beneath power lines of 50,000 volts or less with no load and the boom lowered, the **minimum clearance** between the cab and the line shall be four (4) feet. For 50,000-345,000 volts, the clearance shall be at least ten (10) feet, and for anything greater than 345,000 volts, at least sixteen (16) feet of clearance must be achievable. A **spotter** shall be used to ensure adequate clearance between the lines and the equipment. Boom cage guards, insulating links, and proximity **warning devices** may be used, but the minimum distance must be maintained.

Controls Associated with Compressed Gas Storage and Use

PREVENTING FALLS

If a cylinder falls, it can land on an employee and cause an injury, or the valve assembly could become damaged, which would result in the **uncontrolled release** of high-pressure gas. Such releases can turn the cylinder into a hazardous **projectile** and release the contents into the immediate vicinity.

To reduce the risk of falling, cylinders must be **restrained**, stored in cylinder racks, or mounted on a cylinder cart. Cylinders can be restrained by chains, metal straps, or fire-resistant straps and must be attached to either a structural member or another durable, fixed object to prevent tipping. Cylinder racks are specifically designed to hold and secure cylinders. Cylinder carts are used to move a cylinder between locations and incorporate a restraint into the design to keep the cylinder from falling during transportation.

VALVE COVERS

A **valve cover** is a device that mounts or screws onto a compressed gas cylinder to protect the **valve assembly**. If the valve assembly is damaged, the result can be an uncontrolled release of the cylinder contents. The valve cover must be **durable** enough to protect the valve from damage and **secured** to the cylinder whenever the cylinder is not in use. This will prevent assembly damage in the event the cylinder falls or if the assembly is struck by an object during storage or moving.

STORAGE

Compressed gas cylinders shall be **stored upright** and properly **secured** to prevent falling. Cylinders shall not be stored on **bare earth**, as this can lead to corrosion of the bottom which can lead to failure. **Fuel gas** cylinders must be stored at least twenty (20) feet away from oxygen cylinders or separated by a non-combustible wall at least five (5) feet high and rated for at least thirty (30) minutes of fire protection. Cylinders stored indoors shall be in **well-ventilated** areas or ventilated cabinets and shall not be stored under stairs or near emergency exits.

STORING FUEL GASES AND OXYGEN CYLINDERS IN THE SAME LOCATION

The fire tetrahedron requires fuel, oxygen, heat, and a chain reaction to cause a fire. Some industrial operations require the use of compressed gas cylinders of both oxygen and fuel gas; a good example is welding operations that use oxy-acetylene torches. To reduce the risk of fire and explosion from the storage of these two gases, the National Fire Prevention Association has established two methods for the safe storage of these gases—**separation** by at least twenty (20) feet or by a five (5) foot high **wall** that is fire rated for at least thirty (30) minutes. Only under those conditions can these two gases be stored in the same location.

PREVENTING DAMAGE

Compressed gas cylinders must be protected from failure to prevent fires, exposures, releases, and high-pressure hazards. When cylinders are moved, they are at risk of being dropped or struck by other objects. Cylinders shall only be lifted using **cradles**, **slingboards**, or pallets and may not be moved by a choker sling or magnet, which could allow the cylinder to fall. Cylinders should never be lifted by the valve assembly or moved suspended by an industrial lift. When they need to be moved to a work area, a **cylinder cart** should be used, as this is the safest mode of transporting a compressed gas cylinder of any size.

Basic Industrial Hygiene

Industrial Hygiene

INDUSTRIAL HYGIENE

Industrial hygiene has been described by OSHA as the "science and art devoted to the anticipation, recognition, evaluation, and control" of hazards in the workplace that can cause injury or illness. Where a safety-trained supervisor may use observation as the primary tool for hazard identification, the industrial hygienist will also use analytical tools and instruments to quantify the degree of the hazard. An industrial hygienist will evaluate a workplace for physical, chemical, biological, and ergonomic hazards. Once a hazard has been **identified** and **measured**, the hygienist will then employ the hierarchy of hazard controls to **reduce** the risk of exposure.

CLASSES OF HAZARDS

The role of the industrial hygienist is to **anticipate** and **identify** hazards in the workplace. The goal is to install mitigation **strategies** in an attempt to reduce the risk of impact on workers. The hazards may fall into one of four categories:

- **Chemical** hazards—any hazard caused by a substance or material based on its chemical properties and physical form. Corrosive chemicals that damage the skin, toxic chemicals that damage the liver, or irritants that cause the eyes to water are examples of chemical hazards.
- **Biological** hazards—hazards that are created by living things, including venomous animals, pests, rodents, insects, fungi, molds, and bloodborne pathogens.
- **Physical** hazards—those stressors that impact the body of an individual. This includes noise, pressure, vibration, forces, projectiles, physical injuries (such as cuts, bruises, and fractures), and environmental hazards, including thermal stress.
- **Ergonomic** hazards—workplace design or setup that may result in musculoskeletal disorders (MSD) or repetitive motion injuries (RMI), such as trigger finger or carpal tunnel syndrome.

IDENTIFYING AND CONTROLLING WORKPLACE HAZARDS

Industrial hygienists are charged with **anticipating** and **recognizing** workplace hazards as well as identifying controls for those hazards. Typically, an industrial hygienist (IH) would follow a four-step process to conduct such an assessment:

- **Worksite analysis**—in this first step, the IH would analyze all of the jobs at a location and identify the associated hazards. Walking the location, the IH would observe the work and how it is being done in an attempt to identify the hazards that are present as well as those that may arise in the future. Anticipating future hazards would include forecasting the impact of severe weather or a change in seasons, an increase in staff, or a change in production methods that may introduce hazards into the workplace that are not present during the analysis.
- **Hazard quantification**—in this step, the IH would measure and assign a value to those hazards that can be measured. This would include the use of air monitoring equipment to measure the level of chemicals in the air, a noise monitor to measure the decibels, and video recording of a worker assembling parts to evaluate repetitive motions.
- **Control implementation**—once the hazards are measured and their potential impact is known, the IH will identify appropriate engineering controls, work practices, administrative controls, and personal protective equipment to remove, control, or reduce the risk associated with each hazard.
- **Control evaluation**—in the final step, the IH will monitor the effectiveness of each control and how it has impacted the risk associated with the hazard. If the control is not adequate or does not sufficiently reduce the risk, the IH will implement alternate or additional controls until the risk is at an acceptable level.

DETERMINING LEVEL OF CHEMICAL CONTAMINANTS IN THE AIR

In order to properly control an employee's exposure to a hazardous airborne contaminant, the industrial hygienist needs to determine the **type** and **amount** ("concentration") of contaminant in the environment. Only when the amount of each component is known can the industrial hygienist determine not only if controls need to be implemented but also what control would be effective in reducing the risk to employee health. For example, when selecting a type of respiratory protection, the industrial hygienist needs to know exactly what chemicals are in the breathable air and how much of each constituent to decide between an air-purifying respirator and a supplied-air system.

The two most common methods for measuring air contaminants are grab samples and air monitoring.

- A **grab sample** is when a portion of the atmosphere to be analyzed is pumped into a sample bag or canister. The container is sent to a laboratory to determine what is in the sample and the concentration of each substance that is identified. Sampling provides an accurate and comprehensive evaluation of the environment, but the results are not available until the report is released by the laboratory, and such analyses can be expensive.
- **Air monitoring** is when the atmosphere the employee works in is tested on a continuous basis. Instruments can be attached to an employee ("wearable"), carried by the industrial hygienist ("handheld"), or permanently mounted in a location ("area monitors"). The benefits of air monitoring are in the rapid response time, lower cost, and ability to measure changes as they occur. However, air monitoring instruments tend to be less specific, have a higher degree of error, and may not identify all contaminants in the atmosphere.

Handling and Storing Hazardous Materials or Chemicals

PREVENTING OR CONTAINING HAZARDOUS CHEMICAL SPILLS

Chemicals are ubiquitous in modern workplaces. Production plants may use chemicals as raw materials or produce chemicals as final products. Even office environments have printer toner, cleaning chemicals, paint, window cleaners, and disinfectants, all of which can present a hazard. A **chemical spill** can damage the surrounding environment, make employees sick, or even start a fire. By including measures to **contain and control** spills in the workplace, the employer can reduce the risk of environmental damage and employee injuries.

Proper chemical storage that **segregates** and **separates** chemicals will reduce the risk of leaks and unwanted chemical reactions. Specially designed storage cabinets are made of materials to contain the chemicals and have bottoms to contain spills. Employees should be **trained** on proper storage and handling of chemicals as well as what to do in the event of a spill or when a leak is noticed. Chemical storage areas should be regularly **inspected** to make sure containers are in good condition and not leaking. Finally, **spill kits** should be available to clean up or at least prevent the spread of spill wherever hazardous materials are stored in large volumes.

SEPARATION AND SEGREGATION

Certain materials are **incompatible** with others—if they mix, they react, resulting in a fire, explosion, generation of heat, or production of a toxic by-product. Thus, hazardous materials should be properly segregated and separated in storage locations and during shipping.

Segregation is the process of placing hazardous materials into **categories** based on their properties. Hazard categories include acids, bases, oxidizers, water-reactive, and flammable, to name a few.

Separation is the act of installing a barrier, either a physical barrier such as a wall or distance between incompatible materials, so they cannot come into contact and react. Placing acids in one storage cabinet and bases in another is an example of both segregation and separation.

INCOMPATIBLE

Incompatible can be defined as two things that are unable to exist together. For hazardous materials, this is interpreted as two materials that, when mixed, create a risk to health and safety. Individually, the chemicals may present their own hazards, but when combined they produce another hazard, such as a toxic gas. Chemicals can mix as a result of leaks, misread labels, or accidents during shipping and handling. When two chemicals are described as incompatible, the ensuing reaction can produce **heat** (sometimes at levels high enough to boil water), **fire**, **explosion**, or **toxic** materials. An example of an incompatible reaction would be the generation of hydrogen cyanide gas when sodium cyanide mixes with hydrochloric acid.

CHEMICAL PROTECTIVE ENSEMBLE

A **chemical protective ensemble** is a set of specially designed personal protective equipment (PPE) intended to protect the employee from exposure to chemicals. The ensemble consists of chemical protective garments, boots, gloves, and face protection, which are selected based on the chemicals anticipated to be present during the work activities.

Chemical protective garments are used to protect the arms, legs, and body from chemical exposure. The garments may be separate pieces (such as gowns, sleeves, or coveralls), or they can be a single unit covering the entire body, including attached booties and hoods. The feet are protected from exposure to pooled chemicals or splashes by chemical-resistant **boots**, which typically fit above the calf. Chemical-resistant **gloves** are worn, sometimes multiple pairs, to protect the hands. The face can be protected by chemical splash goggles, a face shield, or a full-face respirator.

CHEMICAL-RESISTANT GLOVES

Chemical-resistant gloves provide a barrier between the hands and hazardous substances. Gloves are available in a variety of materials and thicknesses that are selected based on the chemicals present and their concentration (strength). No one glove will provide adequate protection in all circumstances.

Gloves are available in a variety of **materials**, each of which provides different levels of protection against different classes of materials. Manufacturers prepare glove **selection charts** to allow the employer to select the appropriate material based on the chemicals present in the workplace. For example, poly vinyl alcohol (PVA) gloves provide good protection against halogenated solvents but perform poorly when exposed to acids. Butyl rubber gloves perform well against corrosives (acids and bases) but not so well against some solvents.

In addition to the material, gloves can also have different **thicknesses**. The thicker the glove, the longer it takes a chemical to **permeate** (move through) the material and make its way to the hand. While it may seem logical to always choose a thicker glove, the nature of the task must also be considered because thicker gloves are harder to work in. **Dexterity** decreases with increasing thickness. Thus, the safety professional must not only evaluate the chemical-resistant properties of the glove but also the tasks required, as a loss of dexterity may increase risk of injury or product damage.

Noise Hazards and Controls

NOISE

Noise is a subjective term defined as unwanted or irritating sounds—what is pleasant to one listener may be unpleasant to another.

Occupational noise can create hazards for an employee. Noise can interfere with the ability to communicate and the ability to hear warning or alarm signals. Prolonged exposure to noise has been found to increase psychological stress and can result in a **threshold shift**. A threshold shift is when the **baseline** level of what an employee can hear prior to noise exposure rises over time, indicating a loss of hearing ability. The impact of noise on an employee exposed to high levels of noise is monitored by way of **audiometric tests**—one prior to noise exposure and annually thereafter to identify any potential threshold shifts and related hearing loss.

HEARING CONSERVATION PROGRAM

The Occupational Safety and Health Administration (OSHA) Standard 29 CFR 1910.95 requires a hearing conservation program to be instituted whenever employee exposure to noise exceeds a **time-weighted average** (TWA) of **85 dB** when measured on the A scale. The time-weighted average is measured over an eight-hour workday. This means that the 85 dBA level may occasionally be exceeded as long as the average exposure calculated over an eight-hour time frame does not exceed the action level.

When the TWA exceeds 85 dBA, the employer must implement a **hearing conservation program.** This written program must describe the following:

- How the employer will **monitor** the noise level employees are exposed to
- A means to **notify** employees if they are exposed to potentially hazardous noise
- The audiometric **testing program** to establish a baseline level and evaluate any changes in employees' hearing over time
- The use of **hearing protection** and what will be provided to employees

- The recurring **evaluation** of the effectiveness of the hearing protection devices
- The **training** program for occupational noise exposure

HEARING PROTECTION

The three main types of **hearing protection devices** are earplugs, ear caps, and earmuffs.

- **Foam earplugs** are an inexpensive, disposable type of hearing protection. Foam plugs are designed to be inserted into the ear canal and expand to fit the individual. They do not typically interfere with other protective equipment. However, they can be ineffective if not installed correctly and, if soiled, can introduce dirt into the ear canal.
- **Ear caps** are similar to foam earplugs in their design but are usually attached to a band and are reusable. Where earplugs are easily lost, either singly or in pairs, canal caps can be worn around the neck when not in use. Their effectiveness is dependent on the design of the tips and how deep they fit into the ear canal.
- **Earmuffs** differ from plugs and caps in that they are designed to cover the entire outer ear. They are reusable, can be used by multiple employees, and must be properly cleaned and maintained. Earmuffs are also easier to use effectively than plugs or caps. As they are designed to fit over the ear, there is more interpersonal variability in the shape of the head and ears that can impact the effectiveness of the device. Also, the headbands can interfere with other protective equipment, they are less effective when safety glasses are required, and they are much more cumbersome and heavier than plugs or caps.

ENGINEERING CONTROLS

Whenever employees are exposed to an eight-hour time-weighted average noise level of **85 decibels** or higher, an employer must implement a **hearing conservation program.** Applying the hierarchy of controls, an employer should first use engineering controls in an effort to eliminate the hazardous noise.

In order for noise to be hazardous, the employee must be receiving sound power directly from the source. Power decreases with increasing distance. Thus, **engineering controls** can either interrupt the path of the sound or increase the distance between source and receiver. Enclosing the employee or the noise-producing unit can reduce noise exposure by interrupting the sound wave path. Placing noisy machines or the noisy part of the machine further away from employees also reduces the net sound power they experience. The installation of dampening pads under the machine or sound dampening materials around the machine can also reduce the overall noise.

ADMINISTRATIVE CONTROLS

Administrative hazard controls are located below engineering controls in the hierarchy of hazard controls. Unlike engineering controls which isolate the hazard from the employee, administrative controls look to install **policies and procedures** to reduce the duration of the exposure to an otherwise uncontrolled hazard or can be used in conjunction with engineering controls to further reduce the risk.

For hazardous occupational noise, routine maintenance and repair can ensure that machines are functioning smoothly and reduce the noise they produce. Another method is to reduce the amount of time employees are exposed to noise, such as by job or task rotation, to decrease the effect of noise on their hearing.

OCCUPATIONAL NOISE-INDUCED HEARING LOSS

Exposure to high levels of occupational noise can damage the internal structures of the ear. The duration and extent of the damage are dependent on the **time of exposure, length of exposure,** and **the frequencies** a person is exposed to. The hairs in the ear canal that work with the auditory nerve to perceive sound do not grow back if permanently damaged.

Temporary hearing impacts can include a temporary reduction in hearing that feels as if the ears are stuffed, or **tinnitus** (ringing in the ears). Short-term impacts may resolve by themselves once the employee is removed from the noisy environment.

Long-term hearing impacts are typically irreversible. **Chronic symptoms** can include losing the ability to hear certain frequencies, reduction in ability to understand speech, or permanent ringing in the ears. Exposure to extremely loud and sudden changes in air pressure, such as from an explosion, can rupture the eardrum, resulting in permanent damage.

HAZARDS PRESENTED BY OCCUPATIONAL NOISE

Occupational noise presents multiple hazards to employees. Short-term and long-term exposure can result in temporary or permanent **noise-induced hearing loss**. Impacts can vary from ringing in the ears to threshold shifts where employees lose the ability to hear certain frequencies. Additionally, background noise can impact an employee's **ability to communicate, hear warning signals**, or **hear alarms**. In a noisy environment, an employee may not be able to hear the back-up alarm on a hoist, resulting in an injury. Constant noise is also known to create **stress** for an employee due to the constant bombardment of the auditory system. Noise also interferes with **productivity** and **concentration** for particularly delicate or complicated tasks.

Post-Incident Procedures

POST-INCIDENT STRESS MANAGEMENT PLAN

A workplace accident is **stressful** on everyone involved. First responders, coworkers, associates, and management may all have varying **physical and physiological responses** to the stress that accompanies unusual events. Employers should develop a **post-incident stress management plan** to address this normal response for everyone impacted by the incident:

- **Demobilization**—the first step is intended to allow employees to begin to emotionally **process** the event and **recover**. Immediately after the incident, the responders and those affected should be briefed on the facts of the incident and allowed to ask questions. Care and support should be provided at this point.
- **Defusing**—within the next shift, **professional or trained** individuals should be made available to assist staff in bringing the incident to a conclusion. Individual or small group sessions can help staff work through their feelings, identify immediate needs, and provide support to address the trauma they may have experienced.
- **Debriefing**—within a few days after the event, the entire staff should be convened to discuss the event. This phase is not so much aimed at emotional support as it is to put the event in **perspective**. Additional outcomes from the debriefing may be to provide employees with resources for recovery as each individual processes the event in their own way.
- **Follow-up support**—professional emotional support services should be made available to employees for some time after the event. Some emotional responses may be delayed, and some employees may require longer-term support.

EMPLOYEE ASSISTANCE PROGRAM

An **employee assistance program (EAP)** is an employer-provided **benefit** for short-term counseling, referrals, and follow-up services for employees who have experienced a hardship or trauma. Workplace incidents, including fires, injuries, and fatalities, may trigger **emotional responses** in individuals. Those who rendered aid, knew the victim, or saw the accident may experience symptoms of **post-traumatic stress disorder (PTSD)**. Fires, floods, or major accidents may increase the stress level of employees, including elevated fear of the event happening again. A worker whose friend was involved in a serious workplace accident may feel sadness, anger, or a sense of loss. If assistance is not provided to employees after an incident, the internalized feelings may result in physical or psychological symptoms that impact their work and their lives.

BUSINESS CONTINUITY PLAN

After a major incident, a business needs to return to normal operations as quickly as possible. A **continuity plan** should be designed to recover **critical systems** as quickly as possible. A designated individual or team should be assigned to execute and monitor the process. Any delay in that process can mean a **loss of market share**, loss of **reputation**, or **reduced income**. Critical systems include buildings, utilities, computer systems, personnel, raw materials, customer service, and shipping.

COMPONENTS

Fires, floods, earthquakes, major accidents, pandemics, utility outages, cyberattacks, and public unrest can all interrupt the normal operations of a business. A **business continuity plan** is designed to maintain critical systems during an incident and return operations to a **normal state** as soon as possible once the incident has subsided.

The plan should assign a **designated person or group** who is responsible for executing the plan after an incident. The plan should identify which systems are **critical** and which are non-critical, prioritizing restoration of critical systems. For each identified critical system, the plan should outline who the **responsible party** is for restoring the system and what the criteria are for both minimal operation and restoration to full function. The plan should also identify available **resources**, both internal and external, that can be leveraged for restoring various systems. For example, having a relationship with a professional engineer can facilitate building integrity inspections after a fire, flood, or earthquake. Third-party vendors can assist in restoring IT systems as well as restoring shipping schedules. The plan should be comprehensive, adaptable, realistic, and efficient in order to get the business back on its feet quickly.

Basic Waste Management

RESOURCE CONSERVATION AND RECOVERY ACT (RCRA)

The **Resource Conservation and Recovery Act (RCRA)** is the primary law that governs the disposal of solid and hazardous **waste**. The act gives the Environmental Protection Agency (EPA) the authority to control the fate of hazardous waste from **cradle-to-grave**, meaning from the point of generation to its final disposition. RCRA designates the **roles and responsibilities** for identifying, classifying, packaging, labeling, and transporting waste in a manner that protects the environment. The act provides a list of proper waste codes, describes how to characterize waste, and outlines the training for various roles in the waste management process.

CLASSES OF WASTE

The Environmental Protection Agency (EPA), by way of the **Resource Conservation and Recovery Act (RCRA)**, has designated two main classes of waste—regulated and non-regulated.

A **regulated** waste stream is any waste product that has the potential to harm people or the environment. As a result, the EPA has established **regulations** on how it is to be managed safely to reduce the risk. Categories of regulated waste include hazardous waste, biohazardous waste, medical waste, universal waste, radioactive waste, construction waste, and recycling. **Non-regulated** waste, also referred to as "solid waste," is any waste that is not otherwise regulated. Household garbage is the most common example of solid waste.

CATEGORIES OF UNIVERSAL WASTE

Universal waste is a subcategory of **hazardous waste** that is generated by a variety of businesses. The materials do not require a permit to manage, must be properly labeled, and do not require a Uniform Hazardous Waste Manifest for disposal. Universal waste can be stored on-site for up to one year but must be kept in containers that prevent the hazardous components from escaping into the environment. The EPA has identified five categories of universal waste:

- **Batteries**—including alkaline and rechargeable
- **Pesticides**
- **Lamps**—including fluorescent tubes and LED bulbs
- **Mercury-containing** equipment such as thermostats and light ballasts
- **Aerosol cans**—including partially full cans

UNIFORM HAZARDOUS WASTE MANIFEST

The EPA and DOT have promulgated the use of the **Uniform Hazardous Waste Manifest,** often called simply "manifest," as the primary tracking tool for **hazardous waste** shipments. The manifest is the document that is used to describe the type and record the amount of waste shipped by a generator to a disposal facility. Every party that handles the waste, including the generator, transporter, and final destination facility, must verify the shipment and sign the manifest attesting to what was handled or received. Each party must also retain a **copy** as a record of the waste they managed and the fate of that waste.

The **generator** has the responsibility of properly packaging the waste, classifying the waste, and selecting a destination facility. They generate the manifest, keep a copy, and offer the manifest to the transporter. The transporter **verifies** the shipment and moves the waste from the generator to the final destination. Upon arrival at the **destination facility**, the transporter retains a copy as a record of what was shipped. The destination facility makes a determination as to whether or not it will receive the shipment. Upon agreeing to receive the waste, the facility accepts the manifest and returns a final, signed copy to the generator as proof the waste reached its final destination.

RECYCLING

A material is designated as a **waste** whenever the owner no longer has an intended use for it. The material may be expended, soiled, or never used when it is deemed a waste. **Recycling** is the process of **reducing** the amount of waste that goes into landfills by returning the material into a product chain, either in its current form or in another form. Unused materials can be returned to the supply chain in a process termed "reuse." Expended or soiled materials may find uses in other industries that have different raw material specifications. For example, used ultra-pure solvents may no longer have a use in the semiconductor industry but may be adequate for parts cleaning facilities.

Recycling has the benefits of **reducing the mass** of materials sent to landfills, **conserving** natural resources by providing another source for raw materials, **preventing** pollution associated with new material production, and **conserving** domestic resources by reducing the need to import additional materials.

Hazards Associated with Improper Ergonomics

ERGONOMICS

Ergonomics refers to how the body interacts with the work environment, including tools, equipment, and tasks. From an occupational safety standpoint, ergonomics identifies means to reduce the risk of **musculoskeletal disorders (MSDs)** while still maintaining productivity. MSDs refer to **injuries** to muscles, tendons, joints, and ligaments caused by ergonomic stressors in the environment. **Ergonomic stressors or risk factors** include repetitive motions, awkward positions, and manually moving loads. Examining a job task for these stressors and identifying ways to control them can help prevent musculoskeletal injuries and reduce lost work time.

ERGONOMIC RISK FACTORS

Ergonomic risk factors are those aspects or conditions of a job that can contribute to **biomechanical stress** on the body. It is those elements of the human-work environment interaction that can be reasonably attributed to an **injury**. **Physical risk factors** can include force, posture, repetition, and duration. **Environmental risk factors** can include temperature, light, and noise. Risk factors are hazardous in that chronic exposure can result in cumulative trauma injury, which makes recovery more difficult.

PHYSICAL RISK FACTORS

Ergonomic risk factors are those aspects of the job that negatively impact the body and can result in injury over the long term. These **cumulative trauma injuries** are typically slow in onset and very difficult to recover from without medical intervention. The primary categories for physical ergonomic risk factors are **repetition, force, posture,** and **vibration**.

Repetition is when the body executes the same motion using the same muscles and joints. Repetitive motion can be defined as any motion that has a **cycle time** of less than 30 seconds or is repeated 1,000 times during a shift. The impact is that the body has inadequate time to properly recover, which can result in ligament or tendon damage, including swelling, fraying, or tears.

Force refers to the exertion of physical effort in accomplishing a task. Force can include **lifting, pushing,** and **pulling**. Force can be injurious when the weight being moved exceeds the body's capabilities and muscular or joint injuries occur. Small forces can also be harmful if the motion becomes repetitive. Force can result in strains to the muscles, sprains to ligaments or tendons, and joint damage.

Posture refers to the general body position throughout the work task. **Awkward posture** refers to tasks where the body position is out of neutral alignment. This includes bending, twisting, raising arms above the shoulders, and reaching beyond the center of mass. Posture can also involve prolonged **static tasks** where the body is in one position for an extended period. Sitting and standing are prime examples of a static posture—both of which can be harmful in large doses.

Vibration is the body's repeated exposure to a repetitive force, such as using an impact hammer or driving in a vehicle with bad shocks. The body is constantly being compressed by an external force, which can damage the blood vessels and nerves. This constant compression can result in tissue damage for the affected body part.

MANUAL MATERIALS HANDLING

Manual materials handling is the human activity related to physically moving an object. That motion may be along a horizontal surface (e.g., pushing, pulling), carrying, or lifting/lowering. If not done properly, if done repeatedly without rest, or if the load exceeds what the body is capable of moving, then an injury can result. The following situations can result in a manual materials handling injury:

- Lifting a load from the ground
- Twisting while moving a load
- Lifting a load above the shoulders
- Heavy lifting without assistance
- Repetitive lifting without appropriate rest and recovery

IMPROPER HANDLING INJURIES

Materials handling injuries can result from improper lifting techniques, lifting loads that are too heavy, and awkward postures while lifting (such as reaching or twisting). **Injuries** can include muscle strains, soft tissue sprains, or even soft tissue tears. **Body parts** that can be injured include backs, arms, shoulders, knees, legs, and ankles. Loads that are dropped on an individual can also cause fractures, cuts, or contusions. If improper materials handling techniques are used for long periods of time, such as over a career, the damage to the body may be long-term and irreversible.

AVOIDING MANUAL MATERIALS HANDLING INJURIES

Injuries from manually moving loads can include sprains, strains, and tears of muscles and other soft tissue. In order to reduce the chance of being injured, an employee should perform the following tasks before any lift:

- **Examine** the load for any potential hazards such as slivers, jagged edges, pinch points, or container flaws.
- **Plan** the route of the lift by removing any slip, trip, or fall hazards and ensuring the final resting place is ready to receive the load.
- **Evaluate** the load to determine whether assistance is needed for heavy loads.

- **Locate** proper grip locations and determine whether any gripping devices present are in good condition.
- Make sure they have a **firm grip** on the container and can move the load in their "power zone" (located between the hips and shoulders, at waist level) without blocking their view.
- Avoid moving materials up or down stairs, using ramps or elevators when possible.
- When possible, use carts, dollies, or other mechanical devices for the load.

NIOSH LIFTING EQUATION

A **lift** is defined as moving materials by way of grasping with the hands without mechanical assistance. With manual lifting of loads being a continual source of worker injuries, the National Institute for Occupational Safety and Health (NIOSH) has developed a mathematical equation to assist professionals in assessing the hazard associated with a manual lift.

The **lifting equation** takes into consideration the **distance** the load is carried from the body, the height the load is **lifted** to and from, the height of the load as **carried**, the **frequency** of the lift, the impact of the **grip**, and the amount of **torso twisting** involved. When all of these are considered, the output of the equation is the maximum weight of a load that would be considered "safe." Thus, the resultant value, **Recommended Weight Limit (RWL)**, can be compared to the actual load to be lifted to determine whether other control methods, such as a buddy-lift or mechanical lift device, should be implemented. Once the RWL is calculated, the load weight is divided by the RWL, with the resultant value, the **lifting index (LI)**, determining the relative risk of the lift. An LI value greater than 1 indicates a higher risk of injury associated with the lift.

SEEKING ASSISTANCE

Soft tissue injuries such as strains and sprains, fractures from dropped materials, and slips and trips while walking are all risks from **manual materials handling**. To reduce the chance of injury, employees should request help or find a mechanical means to move a load whenever:

- The load is so **bulky or awkward** that they cannot get a good **grip** on the load, or they cannot lift the load using **proper lifting technique**.
- The employee **cannot see** over or around the load they are carrying, which can cause them to not see walking surface hazards.
- The load exceeds the National Institute of Occupational Safety and Health's (NIOSH) recommended **load limit** for a single individual, which is fifty-one (51) pounds.

INHERENT RISK FACTORS

While an employer can train a worker to avoid muscle and joint injuries and provide ergonomic aids to reduce the risk of injury, there are three main factors the employer cannot control. Those factors are age, physical activity, and strength.

As workers **age**, their ability to recover from ergonomic stressors decreases. Additionally, the longer their career, the longer and more frequently they are exposed to ergonomic stressors. It is well known that muscles lose their elasticity as they age. In younger workers, muscles are more pliable, the number of injuries to any one joint or muscle tend to be fewer, and there has typically been less wear and tear on the tendons and ligaments.

Workers who engage in less **physical activity** have been shown to be more susceptible to musculoskeletal injuries. Those individuals who engage in less physical activity have lower muscle mass, decreased flexibility, decreased strength, and tend to have less coordination than those who are more "fit." All these factors contribute to a higher risk of ergonomic injury.

Strength is the ability to convert muscle energy to work. Workers who have a higher degree of strength will not fatigue as easily, are less susceptible to injury, and their cardiopulmonary system is better suited to doing work for extended periods of time, thereby reducing the risk of a muscle or joint injury.

REPETITIVE MOTION DISORDERS

Repetitive motion disorders (RMDs), as defined by the National Institute of Health (NIH), are soft tissue injuries that are caused by **overuse** of the same muscle group. The continuous and repeated use of the same muscle in the same motion can also negatively impact associated nerves, tendons, and ligaments. Nerves can become irritated, while tendons and ligaments can become inflamed, frayed, or torn. Common RMDs include **carpal tunnel syndrome**, **trigger finger**, and **tennis elbow**. Work tasks that are repetitive include cutting, hammering, typing, packaging, lifting, and material handling.

VIBRATION EXPOSURE

Vibration is when an impact or energy is repeatedly transferred to the body. Under certain conditions, the energy can be transferred from the impact point throughout the body. The part of the body in contact with the vibrating object is subject to repeated compressions and releases. Such continuous, repeated, or long-term compressions can impact the worker's nerves or blood vessels. Equipment associated with vibration injuries includes chain saws, pneumatic hammers, and even vehicles with poorly maintained suspension systems.

Whole-body vibration can cause symptoms such as nausea, fatigue, headache, loss of balance, and shakiness—often resembling motion sickness. Long-term whole-body vibration can cause back problems, circulatory issues, or even impact the bowels. **Hand-arm vibration syndrome** is indicated by numbness, loss of touch, or even blanching (whitening) of the fingers. Continued exposure can affect the worker's grip strength and cause bone cysts.

AWKWARD POSITION

An **awkward position** is any sustained position where the body must move beyond **neutral**. Injuries from awkward positions occur to the muscles and result in strains, while repeated injuries can impact an employee their entire life. Awkward positions include **stooping, kneeling, twisting, stretching,** and **reaching overhead**. Stooping to lift an object off the ground, reaching for an elevated storage location, kneeling to install a computer workstation, and twisting to relocate boxes all expose workers to awkward position injuries. Combinations of these motions, such as kneeling and twisting while restocking inventory, increase the risk of injury.

Environmental Conditions Impacting Worker Health or Safety

THERMAL STRESS

Thermal stress is when the body is unable to maintain its **core temperature** of 98.6 degrees Fahrenheit. The body's physiological systems, such as energy production and organ function, operate effectively and efficiently within a narrow temperature range. If the core body temperature drops below 95 degrees F, a person may start to experience the effects of **hypothermia** or cold stress. If the core body temperature rises above 100 degrees F, they may start to express symptoms of **hyperthermia** or heat stress.

A common misconception is that thermal stress is only a hazard when the outside temperature is either very cold or extremely hot. In truth, cold stress can be brought on by wind which removes body heat very quickly or when a worker gets wet. Heat stress can occur in "comfortable" temperatures if there is high humidity, while using protective clothing, or when an employee works near a heat source, such as a furnace.

HEAT STRESS

Heat stress is a condition when an employee's core body temperature rises above 100 degrees Fahrenheit due to exposure to heat sources, high work rate, or protective clothing. Whenever there is an interruption in the body's ability to **eliminate heat**, due to the weather, work activities, or wearing protective clothing, the employee is at risk of heat stress.

If the body is unable to manage the increase in thermal load, the employee can experience negative physiological effects, termed **hyperthermia**. Heat stress symptoms can vary from mild (heat rash or muscle **cramps**) to fainting (**heat syncope**) to health emergencies (**heat exhaustion and heat stroke**). If the core body temperature exceeds 104 degrees Fahrenheit, the temperature typically associated with heat stroke, the employee may experience brain damage or even die.

COLD STRESS

Cold stress is when an employee's body temperature decreases due to exposure to temperatures lower than room temperature or when the removal of body heat is accelerated. If the body is unable to keep its core temperature within the normal range centered around 98.6 degrees Fahrenheit, the employee can experience negative health effects, termed **hypothermia**. Cold stress can be brought on in cold temperatures, when an employee gets wet, and in windy conditions. Cold stress symptoms can start as shivering, be realized as tingling or discoloration of extremities (**frostbite**), and, if left untreated, progress to loss of consciousness and even death. Cold stress can occur at cool temperatures (as high as 40 degrees F) if an employee gets wet or if there is wind. If the internal body temperature drops below 95 degrees Fahrenheit, the employee may die.

TYPES OF COLD STRESS

Employees who work outdoors in the fall and winter, work in freezers or refrigerators, are exposed to wind, or may get wet are at risk for cold stress. There are three common types of cold stress that employees may encounter—hypothermia, frostbite, and trench foot. **Hypothermia** is when the internal body temperature drops below **95 degrees Fahrenheit**. At this low temperature, the physiological processes necessary to sustain the body start to shut down. Symptoms of hypothermia include shivering, fatigue, and, as the condition worsens, loss of coordination and confusion. **Frostbite** is a condition where the tissue starts to freeze; it is most common in the extremities, such as the hands and feet. **Trench foot** is a condition caused by an extended exposure of the feet to cold and moisture. Trench foot is characterized by red skin, numbness, and blisters, with extreme cases leading to gangrene.

PROTECTIVE CLOTHING AND HEAT STRESS

Protective clothing is designed to provide the worker protection from hazards, such as burns from welding, chemical splashes, or airborne respiratory hazards. Whenever personal protective equipment (PPE) is selected as a control for a hazard, a **barrier** or extra weight is placed on that employee.

Barriers such as welding jackets or chemical protective clothing prevent the body from cooling itself using the **sweating mechanism**. Sweat is supposed to evaporate from the skin, which results in cooling the surface and the blood underneath. If the sweat is kept in contact with the skin, such as in a soaked shirt under a welding jacket, or if it is prevented from evaporating because the employee is wearing a splash-resistant suit, the mechanism fails and the internal body temperature continues to rise.

Additional equipment adds **weight** to an employee, which increases their work rate. Carrying heavy equipment, wearing a self-contained breathing apparatus, or wearing an abrasive blasting suit increases the burden on the heart and increases the amount of **internal heat** that is produced. If this heat cannot be dissipated or is generated faster than it can be released, heat stress can become a concern.

COMBATING HEAT STRESS

There are three main strategies to combat the effect of **heat** on the body—shade, water, and rest. Workers who may be experiencing heat stress should be removed from direct sunlight and allowed to recover in the **shade**. Direct sunlight is one of the contributing factors to heat stress and can increase the body's temperature. When a person experiencing heat stress is moved to the shade, the sun as a source of thermal load is eliminated, and the body can begin to cool. The primary cooling mechanism of the body is evaporative cooling by way of sweating. The **water** lost from perspiring must be replenished, so this system can continue to remain effective in lowering body temperature. Finally, when the body is experiencing thermal stress, the heart is working harder to move blood containing heat from the core to the extremities where cooling is more efficient. If the heart is not allowed to **rest**, negative health effects including dizziness, fainting, and shock can occur.

PHYSICAL EXERTION

The National Institute of Occupational Safety and Health (NIOSH) uses a formula to determine the heat stress a body is experiencing. Heat on a person is calculated using an **environmental factor** and a **metabolic factor**. The environmental factor assesses such things as temperature, humidity, and the impact of direct sunlight. The metabolic factor considers the amount of heat the worker is **generating** by their activity. Muscles burn energy and generate heat as they are used. Therefore, the more muscle groups required or the harder the muscles must work to do the task, the more heat is generated by the body—someone who works harder gets hotter. Work activities are classified as **low, moderate,** and **heavy** in terms of the amount of **exertion** required and the resulting internal heat produced. Thus, employees are more at risk of heat stress when they are doing high-exertion tasks, such as manually moving materials or digging, in moderate conditions or moderate and heavy tasks in high-temperature conditions.

MITIGATION STRATEGIES FOR THERMAL STRESS

Thermal stress can be mitigated by way of engineering controls, administrative controls, and personal protective equipment.

Engineering controls that can address heat stress include the use of air conditioners, fans, or shade structures. Cold stress can be addressed using heaters, insulation, and windscreens.

Administrative controls for temperature stress include rotating workers out of the environment to rest and recover, scheduling tasks for a different part of the day to avoid the stressor, and regularly scheduled breaks. Buddy systems or periodic supervisor checks can be used to monitor employees for signs and symptoms of temperature stress. Lastly, training staff on recognizing temperature stress and how to mitigate the hazard is critical in lowering the chances of a temperature-related injury.

Modern fabrics and advances in clothing design have allowed for a wide selection of both hot and cold weather **personal protective equipment**. Cooling vests, microfiber fabrics, and lightweight clothing can help employees keep cool in hot environments. Advances in cold weather gear, gloves, and footwear can protect employees from injuries caused by cold stress.

When to Seek Assistance in Relation to a Hazard or Situation

COMPETENT PERSON

OSHA defines a construction **competent person** as "one who is capable of **identifying** existing and predictable hazards in the surroundings or working conditions which are unsanitary, hazardous, or dangerous to employees, and who has **authorization** to take prompt **corrective measures** to eliminate them." A competent person gains this knowledge by training, experience, or both. The competent person is also knowledgeable of the relevant standards.

A competent person is required for excavations and trenching, scaffold installation and inspections, rigging inspections, and fall protection. This person is responsible for ensuring all equipment is in proper working condition to avoid failures and that all necessary controls are in place to reduce the risk of injury on the job.

SAFETY PROFESSIONAL

The main role of the **safety professional** is to keep employees safe from injury and illness in the workplace. According to the American Society of Safety Professionals (ASSP), safety professionals have the responsibility to **consult**, **develop** hazard mitigation strategies, and **champion** workplace safety and health initiatives. They can answer questions about potential hazards as well as potential control strategies. The safety professional should always be accessible for any employee question or concern as it relates to the health and safety of the business.

SEEKING OUTSIDE ASSISTANCE

The Code of Ethics for the Board of Certified Safety Professionals states that certified safety professionals should only work within their **area of expertise**. This means that if a safety professional comes across a situation or hazard they are unfamiliar with, they should evaluate their ability to adequately address the situation. If the hazard or control is outside of their **knowledge base**, they should seek outside assistance in the form of **consultants or contractors**. For example, if a safety professional is not familiar with a fall harness, then they should not inspect and certify the devices for use at their company. They should either seek the proper training and certification to increase their knowledge or hire an outside vendor to accomplish the task for them.

Emergency Preparedness and Management

Fire Protection Methods and Classifications

FIRE TETRAHEDRON

The **fire tetrahedron** is the concept that any fire requires four components—**fuel, oxygen, energy,** and a **chemical chain reaction**. Remove any one of the four from the situation and a fire cannot start, or, if it has already started, continue to burn and spread. The foundation of fire prevention is removing or controlling one of the legs. For example, fuels, such as flammable gases or flammable paint thinners, can be safely stored in a space if ignition sources are removed or contained such that they do not come into contact with the fuels. Examples include the use of intrinsically safe switches and light fixtures and prohibiting smoking or open flames in areas where solvents or fuels are stored. Storing oxygen cylinders away from fuel oils or flammable gases is another strategy to eliminate a leg of the tetrahedron.

FIRE TETRAHEDRON AND FIRE SUPPRESSION SYSTEMS

The **fire tetrahedron** concept states that a fire requires four elements to start and to be sustained—fuel, oxygen, energy, and a chemical chain reaction. **Fire suppression** systems look to **eliminate** one or more legs of this tetrahedron to stop the fire or reduce the spread of the flames. For systems that deliver flammable gases or solvents into a process, the fuel can be removed by way of a shutoff valve that is tied to the fire detection system—once an alarm is activated, the **fuel source** is eliminated. Wet fire suppression systems typically use water to remove the **ignition source** or **energy**, since the energy from the flames keeps the fire propagating until the fuel is expended. Water can store a large amount of heat and is intended to remove the energy as a sustainable ignition source.

Oxygen can be removed from burning fuel by dry or inert fire suppression systems in different ways. Systems that use a dry extinguishing agent form a layer on top of the fuel so that the oxygen no longer mixes with the vapors, choking the fire. Inert systems, like those found in computer server rooms, displace oxygen and suffocate the fire by using carbon dioxide or other gas. Finally, specialized chemical agent systems can interrupt the **chain reaction** that sustains a fire, thereby stopping it.

IGNITION SOURCE CONTROLS

Using the concept of the **fire tetrahedron** to combat fire hazards, the risk can be reduced by eliminating the sources of ignition or removing the fuel from the system. If there is no initiating action or no fuel present, a fire cannot start.

Prohibiting smoking and open flames in the work area can prevent embers and discarded cigarettes from starting a fire. Routine **inspection** of electrical appliances, including power strips and extension cords, can reduce the risk of a spark or space

95

heater starting a fire. Appliances that generate **heat**, such as hot plates or toasters, should also be removed from the workplace to minimize fire risk. Wherever flammable liquids are stored, light switches and fixtures should be **intrinsically safe**, so they do not initiate a fire.

FUEL SOURCE CONTROLS

The risk of fire can be mitigated by controlling the fuel leg of the fire tetrahedron. By **limiting** the total amount of fuel, paper products, or other flammable material in any one area, the chance of a fire is reduced as well as the scale of any fire that does start. **Proper storage** of flammable chemicals in specially designed cabinets contains the fuel, limits its access to ignition sources, and provides some protection against flames. Additionally, flammable chemicals should be stored in containers that have spring-loaded lids to keep the vapors contained. Fuels should be **separated** from oxidizing materials that, if mixed with fuels, can ignite by way of a chemical reaction. Finally, general **housekeeping** will keep combustible scrap and materials from piling up and acting as kindling for any sparks or flames.

FIRE EXTINGUISHER FOR AN ELECTRICAL FIRE

A dedicated **Class C** extinguisher is recommended for use on fires that involve energized electrical equipment. This also refers to fires involving portable equipment that is still plugged in. The extinguishing medium must be non-conductive to prevent an electrocution hazard to the individual using the extinguisher.

However, these types of fires can cause surrounding materials to ignite. Thus, a dedicated Class C extinguisher may not be appropriate for the surrounding materials. If a dedicated Class C extinguisher is necessary for delicate electronic equipment, then a supplemental Class A or combination A/B should also be available in the area. Another option is to select a Class A/B/C extinguisher for the area to address all available fuel types.

FLAMMABLE CHEMICAL LIMITS FOR INDOOR STORAGE

One of the methods used to reduce the risk and severity of a fire involving flammable chemicals is to **limit** the volume of flammable materials that can be stored in any one area.

Up to twenty-five (25) gallons of flammable chemicals can be stored indoors without the need for a flammable cabinet. If more than 25 gallons will be present, a specially designed flammable **cabinet** must be used. The maximum amount that can be stored in any one cabinet is sixty (60) gallons of Class 1, Class 2, and Class 3 chemicals combined. For Class 4 chemicals, that limit is increased to one hundred twenty (120) gallons per cabinet. The limit for any single area is three (3) cabinets to reduce the total fuel load.

If more flammable chemicals are required to be stored in an area, then an **indoor storage room** can be used. This room must be **ventilated,** have **intrinsically safe** electrical components, and have an automatic **suppression system**.

MONTHLY PORTABLE FIRE EXTINGUISHER INSPECTIONS

In Standard 10, the National Fire Protection Association (NFPA) establishes the requirements for portable extinguisher inspections. A **portable extinguisher** is any device that is hand-carried or on wheels that contains an extinguishing agent under pressure. NFPA has established two types of inspections—**monthly** and **annual**. The intent of the monthly inspection is to make sure the extinguisher has not been actuated, damaged, or tampered with and is ready in an emergency.

The monthly inspection is a visual inspection and is recorded on the **tag** affixed to the extinguisher by way of the initials of the individual conducting the inspection and the date. The following items must be verified:

- Area around extinguisher has a clear space of no less than 24 inches.
- Pressure gauge is in the operable range.
- The extinguisher contains agent, which is verified by lifting the unit.
- The tamper seal and pin are in place and intact.
- The unit is not visibly damaged

ANNUAL FIRE EXTINGUISHER INSPECTIONS

In addition to the required monthly visual inspections, **fire extinguishers** must also undergo **annual** inspections. The annual inspection shall address all the elements of a monthly inspection as well as the following:

- Operating instructions are present and visible.
- Hydrostatic test has not expired (six-year interval for most extinguishers).
- Pull pin removes from handle.
- All boots, foot rings, and attachments are in good condition and are removed.
- Internal inspection.

Inspection frequency may vary based on the construction of the shell and extinguishing agent. The inspection is **recorded** by replacing and marking the tag attached to the unit with the day, month, and year of the inspection.

CLASSES OF FIRE EXTINGUISHERS

The National Fire Protection Association's Standard 10 identifies five (5) different classes of portable fire extinguishers: **A, B, C, D,** and **K**. Selection of the appropriate extinguisher is based on the **fuel** type(s) present that would contribute to a fire and the amount of combustible material present (fuel load).

- **Class A**: primary fuel is ordinary combustibles, such as wood, paper, or paper-based materials such as cardboard; may be water or a dry chemical extinguishing material.
- **Class B**: the main fuel source for this class is petrochemical products such as flammable liquids, combustible liquids, solvents, alcohols, and flammable gases; extinguishing material can be dry chemical, foam, or carbon dioxide.
- **Class C**: fires that involve energized electrical equipment; extinguishing material is typically dry chemical or carbon dioxide.

97

- **Class D**: this class is used for fires involving flammable metals that burn at very high temperatures such as magnesium, titanium, sodium, and lithium; extinguishing material is dry chemical, typically sodium chloride or graphite.
- **Class K**: this class is used for kitchen fires involving grease and fat; extinguishing material is typically an alkaline mist such as those containing potassium citrate, potassium acetate, or potassium carbonate.

Combination extinguishers, such as A/B, B/C, or A/B/C, can be used in environments where multiple fuel types exist.

LABELING SYSTEM

A portable fire extinguisher is labeled with a **number** and **letter** designation. The letter in a portable fire extinguisher denotes the **fuel type** that the extinguishing agent is effective against. Multiple letters (e.g., A/B/C) indicate a combination extinguisher that can be used for any fuel type on the label.

The number is the **size rating** of the extinguishing agent and is dependent upon the fuel type of the extinguisher.

- For a Type A extinguisher, the number describes the **water equivalency** of the extinguishing agent. Each number represents an amount of extinguishing agent **equivalent to a gallon and a quarter** of water. Thus, an extinguisher labeled as "2A" has enough extinguishing agent to equal two and a half gallons of water; a "4" would be equivalent to five gallons of water.
- For a Type B extinguisher, the number describes the **square footage** that the agent can cover if continually held and moved side to side. Thus, a 40B can cover 40 square feet.
- Thus, an extinguisher that is rated 4A:20B has a water equivalency for Type A fires of 5 gallons and can cover 20 square feet for a flammable liquid fire.
- Types C and D do not have an equivalent size rating.

FIXED WATER-BASED FIRE SUPPRESSION SYSTEMS

A fixed fire **suppression system** consists of a detection system that activates a permanently mounted suppression system. There are two broad classes of fixed suppression systems—wet pipe and dry pipe.

In **wet pipe** systems, the sprinkler pipes and lines are always filled with **water**. When the detection system signals system activation, water is **immediately** supplied through the sprinkler heads. For a **dry pipe** system, the lines are filled with **compressed air**. The air pressure is maintained by a compressor, nitrogen tanks, or other means. Upon activation, the air escapes through the sprinkler heads, followed by water. Dry pipe systems are designed for locations where subfreezing temperatures may cause water-filled pipes to crack or burst.

FIRE PROTECTION SYSTEM

A **fire protection system** is designed to limit the damage caused by fire and protect both life and property. A system has four main components—detection, initiation, notification, and suppression.

The **detection system** is used to identify the presence of combustion as soon as possible. The system can be composed of three types of detectors—heat detectors, ionization smoke detectors, or photoelectric smoke detectors. The detectors are connected to a fire panel and the initiation system to deploy fire suppression agents as soon as possible.

The **initiation system** triggers the fire suppression system to release the agent used to extinguish the fire. There are two types of initiators—manual and automatic. **Manual** initiators require the direct action of a person, such as fire alarm pull stations. **Automatic** initiators are integrated with the detectors that sense fire, smoke, or heat and activate the suppression system.

The **notification system** is used to convey either a system activation or, in the case of inert gas systems, an impending system discharge. Inert systems push oxygen out of a room and must warn occupants to evacuate prior to the suppression system activating. The notification consists of both visual and audible **indicators** to notify occupants of the need to leave.

The **suppression system** is a series of pipes and discharge devices that release the extinguishing agent in the area to extinguish a fire. Suppression systems may be water-based, clean agent, foam, or dry chemical systems.

CLEAN AGENT FIRE SUPPRESSION SYSTEM

The National Fire Prevention Association (NFPA) describes a **clean agent** fire suppression system as an extinguishing system that uses a **non-conducting gas** or very **low boiling agent** which does not leave a **residue** once the system has been activated. Clean agent systems are not water-based and can be used on Class A, B, or C fires. They are the preferred system for use in and around electronic systems, including computer server rooms. Unlike water-based, dry agent, or foam systems, there is no cleanup required after system discharge. The agents work by starving the fire of oxygen, thereby interrupting the fire tetrahedron. The most commonly deployed gases for clean agents are carbon dioxide, nitrogen, and argon.

PHYSICAL ATTRIBUTES OF A FUEL

A fire needs oxygen, energy, a chemical reaction, and fuel to propagate. In terms of the **fuel**, it is not the actual liquid or solid that burns but the **vapors** above the fuel that are generated by heat. Fuels that evaporate more readily can easily form a flammable mixture with air. The ability of a fuel to **evaporate** is directly related to the chemical property of **boiling point**. The temperature at which enough fuel has evaporated into the air to form a flammable mixture is termed the **flashpoint**. In terms of risk, fuels with lower boiling points and lower flashpoints are more hazardous. NFPA 30 lists three classes of fuels:

- **Class I**: **flammable** liquids having flashpoints below 100 °F (37.8 °C). Class I is further subdivided as IA (flashpoint below 73 °F (22.8 °C) and a boiling point below 100 °F), IB (flashpoint below 73 °F and a boiling point at or above 100 °F), and IC (flashpoint between 73 and 100 °F).
- **Class II**: **combustible** liquids having flashpoints above 100 °F and below 140 °F (60 °C).
- **Class III**: **combustible** liquids having flashpoints at or above 140 °F (60 °C); subdivided into IIIA (flashpoint between 140 and 200 °F (93°C)) and IIIB (above 200 °F).

LEL, UEL, LFL, AND UFL

Fuels require a certain amount of **oxygen** to burn. For each fuel, there is a range of fuel-to-oxygen mixtures where burning can occur. This is termed the **flammable range**.

When there is not enough oxygen for a fuel to ignite or combust, the mixture is referred to as "too lean." The concentration below which there is not enough fuel in the mixture (too much oxygen) is called the **lower flammable limit (LFL).** If the fuel is contained in a small area where ignition would result in an explosion, the level is called the **lower explosive limit (LEL).** Conversely, if there is too much fuel and not enough oxygen, the mixture is termed "too rich" to burn. The highest amount of fuel in an area that can ignite is termed the **upper flammable limit (UFL)** or **upper explosive limit (UEL)**.

Fire Safety Requirements

NATIONAL FIRE PREVENTION ASSOCIATION (NFPA)

The **National Fire Prevention Association (NFPA)** is a global nonprofit organization dedicated to reducing the loss of life and property damage due to fires. Established in 1896, the NFPA currently develops and publishes **codes** on various topics related to fire safety. These codes address such topics as the performance requirements of fire suppression systems, the inspection frequency for fire extinguishers, specifications for emergency exits, and proper storage of flammable chemicals. NFPA publishes their codes online at no cost as a reference for concerned parties. Many of their codes are incorporated into OSHA regulations by reference and adopted by local or state fire agencies.

FIRE INSPECTION CHECKLIST

A **fire inspection checklist** can be used by supervisors or safety personnel to identify potential **fire hazards** and whether adequate **controls** exist. The checklist should be used to reduce the opportunity for a fire and improve the ability to suppress any fire that starts.

To protect employees, the checklist should include ensuring that **egress** pathways are clear and **exits** are not obstructed. In terms of preventing fires from starting, the inspection should address **electrical hazards** to make sure that cords are intact, circuits are not overloaded, and electrical devices are properly safeguarded. **Fuel sources** should be assessed by making sure that the fuel load in any one area is minimized by restricting the amount of flammable chemicals, paper products, or other combustible materials. Additionally, flammable materials should not be stored close to ceilings, where they can propagate a fire. **Housekeeping** should be evaluated to both remove potential fuels and maintain safety evacuation pathways. Finally, the **fire system components** should be inspected, including alarms, detectors, and extinguishing systems.

INSPECTING A FIRE SUPPRESSION SYSTEMS

The **building owner or occupant** is responsible for making sure the **fire suppression system** will protect the structure in the event of a fire. Often, the building's owner and the business's insurers will require **regular inspections** to reduce their exposure to a loss due to fire. The employer may have an employee who is properly trained conduct the inspections or an outside, certified contractor may be used. The inspector must be aware of the requirements for all systems as well as the **frequency** of inspections, which is different for the various system components.

FLAMMABLE LIQUID STORAGE CONTAINERS

Flammable liquids present a fire hazard in that they serve as a fuel source. It is not unusual to consolidate flammable liquid containers into a single cabinet or area. This increases fire risk since if one container catches fire, there is a good chance the rest of them will. The hazard lies in the **vapor**—the gaseous form of the fuel that evaporates and can fill an enclosed space. Additionally, if a container fails and the liquid is released, a fire can spread quickly and easily. Thus, containers for flammable liquids must be designed to prevent the start or propagation of a fire.

If the amount used and stored is one gallon or less, the original container can be used. For more than one (1) gallon but less than five (5), **safety cans** must be used. A safety can has a **spring-loaded lid,** a **vent,** and a **flame arrester** to prevent the vapors from catching fire. Containers should be of glass or metal construction, as plastic containers can hold static charges that, if discharged, can act as an ignition source.

FLAMMABLE CHEMICAL STORAGE CABINET

When more than 25 gallons of flammable liquids must be stored in a single area, a compliant **flammable storage cabinet** must be used. Per 29 CFR 1910.106, the cabinet must:

- Be **fire-resistant** to maintain an internal cabinet temperature of less than 325 degrees Fahrenheit for at least 10 minutes
- Be clearly **labeled** "Flammable—Keep Fire Away" or a similar warning

- If constructed of metal, be at least 18-gauge steel with **tight seams** and have **double-walls** with at least ½ inch of air space with a **three-point lock** and a bottom **lip** of at least 2 inches
- If constructed of wood, be made of fire-resistant plywood at least 1 inch thick and have rabbeted joints secured with screws, overlapping doors, and hinges that resist losing their ability to hold the doors when exposed to flames

PASS PROCESS

PASS is an acronym that describes how to use a **portable fire extinguisher**. The process works as follows:

- **Pull** the pin. Each portable fire extinguisher has a pin to prevent an accidental discharge of the extinguishing agent.
- **Aim**. One hand is used to hold the extinguisher handle while the other holds the hose. The end of the hose should be aimed to discharge extinguishing agent at the base of the flame.
- **Squeeze**. The extinguishing agent is discharged when the handle is squeezed, taking care not to pinch the user's hand or fingers.
- **Sweep**. As the agent is being discharged, the hose is swept back and forth, over a larger area than the spread of the flame, to extinguish the fire.

NFPA 704 HAZARD IDENTIFICATION SYSTEM

The National Fire Prevention Association publishes **Standard 704**, "Standard System for the Identification of the Hazards of Materials for Emergency Response." This system uses a color and numbering system as a quick indicator of the **chemical hazards** that are present at any one location. The system is intended to provide first responders with general hazard information to assist in their response planning.

The system arranges four **colored blocks** in a diamond pattern. The colors red, white, yellow, and blue each represent a hazard presented by chemicals stored at a location. Red (top of diamond) indicates **flammability**; white (bottom of diamond) indicates **special** hazards (like oxidizers); yellow (right side of diamond) indicates chemical **reactivity**; and blue (left side of diamond) indicates **health** hazards. The general level of hazard is indicated using numbers ranging from 0 to 4 (0 = lowest and 4 = highest).

OCCUPANCY

The requirements for emergency escapes, fire suppression systems, and fire prevention programs are dependent on a building's **occupancy class**. The occupancy, identified by letters such as "Class B" and "Class M," generally describes the **intended use** of a building. For example, a Class H (high hazard) building where flammable solvents are used in large amounts has different requirements than a school (Class E) or a movie theater (Class A). The fire and life safety systems and requirements vary by class based on the anticipated hazards, processes, use, and occupation density.

EMERGENCY EXITS

The National Fire Prevention Association promulgates the Life Safety Code, Standard 101. Among other items, this standard outlines the requirements for safely and effectively evacuating people from a building during an emergency. The Life Safety Code describes the three components of an **emergency exit**:

- **Exit access**—the portion of an exit route that leads to the exit, including the vestibule and pathway, including allowable widths, signage, and lighting; an example of an exit access would be the hallway that leads to the exit door.
- **Exit**—this portion is the actual portal that leads from one area to another—it is the gateway from the access to the discharge; a 2-hour rated fire door would be an "exit."
- **Exit discharge**—once people pass through the exit, they enter the exit discharge area, which is the area that leads them from the building to an area of safety; this would be the area on the other side of the exit door, where people are officially out of the structure.

VISUAL FIRE ALARMS

Visual fire alarm indicators are required in response to the Americans with Disabilities Act (ADA), so individuals who are **hearing impaired** will be notified of an active alarm situation. NFPA has established criteria for visual fire alarms by way of NFPA 72. This standard requires that visual alarms be **clear or white** and flash between **1-2 times per second**. If there are more than two visual indicators in any room, the strobes must be **synchronized** to flash simultaneously.

AUDIBLE FIRE ALARMS

An **audible fire alarm** is considered a public alarm and is designed to notify everyone within a specific area. Per NFPA 72, the audible signal must be at least **15 dBA above** the noise level typically present in the facility. Additionally, the alarm must be of a different **tone** than other notification systems within the building, so employees can discriminate between process indicators and the need to evacuate.

EMERGENCY EXIT SIGNAGE

An **emergency exit** is a specially designated egress route that directs evacuating employees along a safe path out of the building. 29 CFR 1910.37 outlines the requirements for identifying the location of designated exits. The **door** must be clearly labeled "Exit," and the sign must be **illuminated**. The sign can either be luminescent or powered by a battery backup such that the sign is visible if the area lighting is impacted by the emergency. The exit signs must be a distinct **color**, and the **letters** must be at least 6 inches high and at least ¾ inch in width. Any door along the exit access (pathway) that could be mistaken for an exit must be clearly marked "not an exit." Local fire jurisdictions may have additional requirements.

EMERGENCY ESCAPE ROUTE LIGHTING

In some emergency situations, the power to the building may be impacted. **Emergency lighting**, also referred to as **egress lighting**, is intended to illuminate the escape route to allow for a safe and organized building evacuation even in the event of a loss of power. Egress lighting systems must be present in hallways, stairwells, and exits designated as evacuation routes. The NFPA's Life Safety Code outlines the requirements for emergency egress illumination, including:

- A minimum of **1.5 hours** of illumination upon loss of power to the building
- Minimum and maximum **brightness** levels
- Must turn on **automatically** in the event of a power failure
- Monthly and annual **testing**

Emergency Response Plans and Drills

EMPLOYEE FIRE SAFETY TRAINING PROGRAM

An effective **fire safety training** program should prepare employees for an emergency by **informing** them of their responsibilities and outlining the actions that should be taken. The program should include **fire prevention strategies** based on the fire tetrahedron. Such strategies should address housekeeping, sources of ignition, and processes to reduce the risk of fire. Training should also describe the **actions** an employee should take during a fire emergency. The employer must decide how they want their employees to **respond** and whether they should attempt to put out small fires or simply evacuate. An employer may also choose to train groups of employees for different response levels, such as a fire brigade, first responders, and employees who will simply evacuate. Finally, in order to prevent small (incipient) fires from becoming large, the fire safety training should include teaching employees how to use **portable fire extinguishers** safely and effectively.

EMERGENCY RESPONSE

The Federal Emergency Management Administration (FEMA) has identified four phases of an **emergency response**—mitigation, preparedness, response, and recovery. **Mitigation** is the phase when actions are taken to **reduce** the risk, impact, and results of an emergency event. Mitigating actions include purchasing insurance policies, installing seismic bracing, and inspecting fire suppression systems. In the **preparedness** phase, the employer **develops** their emergency action plan and **trains** employees how to respond in an emergency situation. This phase also includes site evaluations to identify areas of vulnerability. The **response** phase is when actions are taken **during and immediately after** an emergency event. Executing the emergency action plan, accounting for employees, and contacting first responders are part of this third phase. The fourth phase is **recovery**, wherein the business begins to **return** to normal operations. During recovery, employees are allowed back into the building, systems are restored, and necessary repairs are conducted. In this FEMA model, the phases exist as a continuous loop to remain prepared for any unexpected event.

WORKPLACE EMERGENCY

An **emergency** is an unexpected condition or event that disrupts normal operations. At a construction site, this could include a fire, chemical spill, or accident.

Emergencies can be **natural** or **man-made**. Natural emergencies include earthquakes, floods, hurricanes, and tornadoes. Man-made emergencies include arson, terrorism, active shooters, and industrial accidents.

Emergencies can endanger workers, interrupt project timelines, destroy property or materials, and shut down operations completely. Unexpected events can result in **injuries** or **illnesses** to employees, which can impact the size and availability of the workforce. Emergencies cannot be predicted, but plans can be put in place to reduce their impact on the project.

EMERGENCY ACTION PLAN

OSHA describes the required elements of an **emergency action plan** when one is required by the operations at the site. The written plan must include:

- **Emergency escape** procedures, including escape routes
- Procedures for any employees who must operate or shut down **critical operations** prior to evacuating
- A method to **account** for all employees after an evacuation
- **Rescue and medical procedures** for any employees who are assigned to those duties
- Means of **reporting** emergencies, such as fire and medical events
- Names and job titles of those **responsible** for answering employee questions about the plan

A **written** copy of the plan must be available to any employee who wants to review it.

EMERGENCY ACTION PLAN TRAINING

Training on the emergency action plan is used to make sure that all employees receive the information on what to do in the event of an emergency, such as a fire or hazardous material spill. All employees must be **trained** when the plan is implemented. Employees must receive information on all elements of the plan, including **alarm signals, evacuation routes,** and **assembly areas**. Employees must receive additional training whenever the plan is **changed** and it affects their operations. Individual employees must receive updated information whenever they **change assignments** and elements of the plan that impact them are different, such as their evacuation route and assembly area.

EMERGENCY ACTION PLAN VS. EMERGENCY RESPONSE PLAN

Planning for emergencies is critical for any business to **prevent** injuries, **reduce** losses, and **resume** operations as soon as possible. During an emergency is not the appropriate time to figure out what to do and who is responsible. There are two types of plans typically required by regulatory agencies—an **Emergency Action Plan (EAP)** and an **Emergency Response Plan (ERP)**.

An EAP is typically **defensive** in nature. It describes how an employer will evacuate, where people will meet, how they will communicate with responding agencies, and how they will account for everyone. An EAP can be applied to a **variety** of emergencies, including medical emergencies, active shooters, fires, earthquakes, and floods.

An ERP is used when an employer will **take action** to address the emergency. Whether it is for a hazardous material spill or a fire, an ERP delineates **specific** response elements for a particular emergency. The ERP will **designate** responders, outline their **training**, describe **alarm systems**, explain the **equipment** required for a response, outline how the team will **integrate** with external agencies (e.g., fire or medical), and include a provision to **review** any responses for future improvement.

EMERGENCY RESPONSE PLAN

An **emergency response plan (ERP)** is the employer's process for responding to the unintended release of a hazardous material. The ERP can be part of an organization's **contingency plan** but differs in that it is specific for those employers who will have employees respond to the release in some fashion. The extent of the program and training required for staff under the Hazardous Waste Operations and Emergency Response Standard (HAZWOPER) (29 CFR 1910.120) will depend on whether employees will simply prevent entry to the area where the release occurred or actively try to stop the release, leak, or spill.

At a minimum, ERPs should include:

- Pre-emergency **planning and coordination** with local emergency response agencies
- **Identifying** staff who will respond to the spill and their required **training**
- How staff will **recognize** a release and the **actions** they are to take
- Establishing safe distances and places of refuge
- How **site security** will be established and maintained during emergency activities
- **Decontamination procedures** for contaminated staff and emergency responders
- Emergency **medical treatment and first aid**, including coordination with local hospitals
- The procedures used to **alert** staff and initiate a response
- A method for **post-response critique** for continual improvement

EMERGENCY RESPONSE PLAN PREPARATION

If a project requires that hazardous materials are stored or used on-site, the employer must prepare an **emergency response plan** to reduce any potential harm that may be caused by a chemical release. The ability to quickly respond and stabilize an emergency requires planning, practicing, evaluating, and adjusting.

- **Planning**—creating an emergency response plan in advance of an emergency is critical in managing the event. Planning allows for establishing **roles and responsibilities** as well as allowing the company to procure necessary materials before they are needed. The overall goal of planning is to reduce the time between event and mitigation to reduce losses.
- **Practicing**—response team members must learn to use equipment, ask questions about their role, and troubleshoot the response plan elements before an actual emergency occurs. **Practicing and training** is the most effective method for team members to learn to work together without the stress of a real emergency.
- **Evaluating**—the effectiveness of a plan must be continually evaluated. Practicing an emergency response allows the team to identify **areas for improvement** before an emergency occurs. Robust plans are also evaluated after an emergency response. Evaluation should include identifying aspects that worked well, areas that can be improved, and things that failed to work as designed.
- **Adjusting**—the plan should be adjusted whenever improvements are identified. Response activities that worked well can be expanded to other aspects of the response. Areas that need correction can be adjusted and then practiced again to determine whether the performance goals were achieved.

EVACUATION DRILLS

The National Fire Prevention Association (NFPA) Standard 1 establishes the provisions for **evacuation drills**. Drills must:

- be held with **sufficient frequency** to familiarize occupants with the process (typically at least annually),
- be managed in an **orderly and organized** fashion to convey individual responsibilities during a true emergency and not purely focused on speed of egress,
- not be held always at the same time and manner to better **resemble an actual event**,
- identify a **relocation area** to allow for all occupants to be accounted for, and
- be **documented** by way of a record noting the date, time, and type of drill.

RESPONDING TO CHEMICAL SPILLS

Every emergency response should be focused on **preventing** as many injuries as possible and **containing** the situation. Under this premise, an employee should be trained to respond to a chemical spill as follows:

- The safety of those in the immediate area of the spill must be ensured by **evacuating** them to reduce the risk of exposure and injury.
- The area of the spill or release should be **isolated**, so no additional employees have the potential for exposure.
- The proper **notification** must be made to initiate a response, as described in the employer's emergency response plan.

CONVEYING EMERGENCY PLAN TO EMPLOYEES

All employees, contractors, subcontractors, and vendors at a job site must be **aware** of the actions they are to take in the event of an emergency. These groups can be informed of their responsibilities and evacuation procedures by short briefings, formal trainings, or printed materials.

Visitors and subcontractors can be given a brief **oral presentation** on the emergency procedures, location of emergency equipment, and evacuation routes. If the plan is more complex based on site activities, the information can be relayed by **formal training** in a classroom setting. This method is appropriate for employees who will have specific roles, such as chemical spill responders, medical responders, and fire brigades. In place of oral presentations, the information may be presented in the form of **written materials** that can be handed out to employees. Supervisors should review the written information, so everyone knows how to evacuate safely if the need arises.

Ethical Leadership

Professional and Organizational Ethics

ETHICS

Ethics can be defined as the standards of what is right and what is wrong. As a set of **moral principles**, ethics guide the decisions a person makes in an effort to benefit both individuals and society. Ethics impact an individual's approach to problems, challenges, and interpersonal relationships. When applied to a business, ethics can be framed by the leader of an organization as the expectations of behavior for employees who represent the business and its interests. These expectations are often set forth by way of a **code of ethics**.

CODE OF ETHICS

A code of ethics is a **written** document that lists the **principles of conduct** expected of the members of the body. Those principles guide **decision-making**, establish expectations for **behavior**, and act as a **standard of practice** for members. For example, the Code of Ethics for the Board of Certified Safety Professionals lists eight principles that it demands of certified members to promulgate the integrity, honor, and prestige of the profession. By outlining the principles in a documented fashion, the body explicitly establishes how it expects its members to behave.

ETHICAL BEHAVIOR

Ethical behavior is when a person acts with honesty, fairness, and equity while interacting with others. A person who acts ethically respects the fact that others may have differences in beliefs or opinions and that those opinions have **equal value**. Additionally, ethical behavior implies that a person will act in the best interest of all stakeholders and not just their own. Ethical behavior can have a **positive impact** on an organization's relationships, reputation, and employee retention.

PROFESSIONAL CODE OF ETHICS

A professional code of ethics is a **written document** that establishes the expectations of all members of that professional group. In addition to describing the organization's **mission** and **values**, the document outlines how the organization expects its members to approach problems and choose between what is right and what is wrong. Thus, any individual certified by a professional body is expected to know and adhere to its code of ethics.

Not only does the document outline expectations, but it can also be used as a metric to **judge** members who may have acted inappropriately. If a member of a professional society is determined to have violated the organization's ethical code, the member could be dismissed from the group and lose all associated rights and privileges, including their certification.

ETHICAL RESPONSIBILITY OF SAFETY PROFESSIONALS

The safety professional must demonstrate ethical behavior at all times. This means that, even when faced with the **competing priorities** of management, they must do what is **right** and follow the regulations. Compromising safety in order to shorten a timeline or reduce project cost is never worth the risk to an employee's safety. Safety professionals have a responsibility to **protect life** and **property**. They are beholden to the greater good of the health and safety of the employees and must keep that at the forefront of their decision-making process.

In business there is often a **fiscal motivation** to complete projects quicker or cheaper. The safety professional must continually lobby that health and safety be **prioritized** and not compromised to meet those goals. The safety professional must **communicate** to management the potential costs of cutting safety—accidents result in delays, impact production, and have both hard and soft costs. Accidents can also negatively impact the **morale** of the entire project team, which can affect quality and productivity. Thus, no matter how difficult it may be, safety professionals must always stress the need for safety and not compromise their ethical responsibility to the employees.

MAINTAINING TRAINING RECORDS

Organizations will maintain a variety of records, including health and safety **training records** that demonstrate compliance with applicable regulations. Thus, recordkeeping for an organization must be done ethically.

The integrity of these files is paramount in maintaining the **truthfulness** of the information contained within. These records must accurately reflect both the training and the attendees. Unethical recordkeeping, such as forging training attendance records, ultimately endangers employees. If a record shows that an employee attended a training when they did not, they are not receiving the information they need to work safely. This puts the employee at risk for injury and the company at risk for not only negligent behavior but the consequences of intentionally forging records.

CODE OF ETHICS VIOLATION

Professional certification boards, such as the Board of Certified Safety Professionals (BCSP), will adopt a **code of ethics** to outline the expected behavior of those individuals they certify. Any person, member or nonmember, who believes that a safety professional certified by BCSP has violated the code of ethics may report the infraction. The BCSP has adopted a **disciplinary policy** that allows it to revoke a member's credential if they are found to have violated the adopted code of ethics. The formal **proceeding** includes a hearing by the Judicial Commission, and if a serious violation is deemed to have occurred, the individual may have their credential permanently revoked.

BCSP Code of Ethics

PRINCIPLES

A **principle** is a basic **moral belief** that guides conduct and behavior. In its plural form, it has been defined as a list of values. Thus, when a person has principles, it means they have a moral code that guides their actions. Principles are **universally** applicable, not bound to a specific group or set of beliefs. Examples of principles that apply to everyone include honesty, fairness, and integrity. While ethics are defined by and applied to a specific group, principles apply to all.

PRINCIPLES AND SAFETY PROFESSIONALS

Principles are universally applicable morals that guide behavior. A safety professional must adhere to a set of principles that guides their decision-making at all times. Safety may appear to impede or interfere with an organization's business goals and objectives. Implementing proper safety measures, conducting trainings, and doing required inspections can seem to slow down the project and negatively impact timelines and deadlines. However, the safety professional cannot compromise their principles to appease management or the bookkeeper. The safety professional must reinforce that an inspection takes much less time than an accident investigation, that the cost of an injury is greater than the expense of installing a machine guard. If the professional does not **uphold** their principles and begins to take shortcuts or eliminate statutory requirements to satisfy management, they will soon lose the respect of those they are trying to protect, resulting in ignored initiatives and wasted efforts.

PRINCIPLES AND CODE OF ETHICS

A code of ethics is a **document** that outlines the expected behavior of those affiliated with a particular organization. This code will provide a roadmap for how the affiliates are to make decisions, interact with others, and prioritize initiatives within the organization. In order to direct behavior, the code typically comprises a set of **principles** that explicitly outline the expectations for individuals. The code attempts to **align** individuals into a singular moral base, so the company has a common set of rules for doing business.

BCSP CODE OF ETHICS

The **Board of Certified Safety Professionals (BCSP)®** expects all persons who have achieved certification under their programs to adhere to the following eight (8) principles outlined in their **code of ethics**:

- Protect the safety of others, protect the environment, protect property, and discourage those they consult from taking risks that can imperil any of those.
- Act with integrity, avoid bias, and not be swayed by the client or try to appease the public.
- Only issue public statements that are truthful and based in fact.
- Not work outside of their knowledge base and continually pursue professional development.

- Not misrepresent their qualifications or falsify their past work.
- Avoid conflicts of interest.
- Avoid discrimination in all forms.
- Always work for the advancement of the safety profession.

LEADERSHIP

ETHICAL LEADERSHIP

Ethical leadership is when those in decision-making positions demonstrate the **expected** and **appropriate conduct** for subordinates. In basic terms, the individual leads by **example**. For a safety professional, this means adhering to safety requirements at all times while at the worksite—wearing the appropriate personal protective equipment, following the procedures, and abiding by all safety regulations.

Ethical leadership is achieved by **mutual respect** and two-way communication. Safety leadership is not accomplished by threats or strong-arm tactics. It is accomplished by **humanizing** the employees and **building relationships**. Rules are applied evenly, as are expectations—there are no "favorites" nor turning a blind eye. This approach has been shown to be much more effective at creating a positive safety culture within an organization.

LEADERSHIP

Leadership can be defined as the act of leading a group of people. A leader **influences and motivates** others to move in a coordinated direction toward the achievement of an organization's goals. This influence is achieved by demonstrating a concern for the well-being of others and meeting their needs. Those needs may be financial, such as providing a paycheck, or moral, such as when workers are given a means of achieving internal fulfillment.

SAFETY LEADERSHIP

A leader motivates and inspires others to follow them toward a specified goal. The role of a safety professional is to assume the responsibility of **safety leadership** within an organization. This entails consistently **following** safety procedures and protocols, such as always wearing protective equipment when it is required. A safety leader **champions** safety in all aspects of the organization, making an effort to **recognize** those who are working safely and assist those who are not.

The safety leader is charged with **identifying** the desired state of the safety management system, **establishing** the policies and procedures to achieve the desired state, and **encouraging** the stakeholders during the journey. The safety leader establishes the expectations for employee behavior and **provides** the tools, such as equipment and training, to encourage safe decisions and actions. Ultimately, the success of any safety management system is dependent on good safety leadership.

INTEGRITY

Integrity can be defined as the **adherence** to an ethical or moral code. It is the practice of being **honest** and doing what is right, no matter the circumstances. Integrity is difficult to establish but easy to lose.

Integrity is multifaceted. It is demonstrated by **following through** on promises to locate information, **avoiding** gossip, and being **fair** and **consistent**. It also involves putting aside personal gain for the advancement of the organization.

INTEGRITY IN THE SAFETY PROFESSION

Integrity is a quality of a successful leader. A safety professional is part of the leadership team, even if they are not part of the management team. Their role is to **convince** employees to follow safe procedures and protocols, use protective equipment, and avoid risky behaviors. In some instances, the safety professional must manage the **change** from a risky culture to a risk-averse culture.

The safety professional must demonstrate integrity by adhering to health and safety measures at all times to avoid seeming hypocritical. Managers must be held to the same safety standards as all others, so employees can see that the safety professional is fair and consistent, regardless of status. When the safety professional has earned the **confidence** of a group of employees, they will be more willing to listen, follow, and support safety initiatives. The safety professional must believe in safety and the **importance** of the worker in order to be successful. The integrity of the safety professional plays an important role in that success.

COMPROMISING INTEGRITY

Integrity is the personal aspect of always adhering to a moral or ethical code, regardless of the context or circumstances. Safety professionals must always demonstrate integrity to retain belief in their intent and strive to be a safety leader. Unfortunately, integrity is challenging to establish but easy to lose.

A safety professional can compromise their integrity if they have a **bias** or play favorites. Not reprimanding a person for a safety violation because they are a friend outside of work will demonstrate to other employees that the rules are not applied equally. Another example would be completing inspection logs without having walked the site. A safety professional who is perceived as **dishonest** will not be trusted by others to maintain confidentiality, which may impact their willingness to report potential violations. Finally, if a safety professional **ignores** the input or opinions of others, they will be seen as lacking integrity. If an employee does not feel valued, they will not have faith that the safety professional has their best interests in mind.

DIVERSITY AND BIAS

DIVERSITY

Diversity is the understanding and acknowledgment that each person is **unique**, and everyone has their differences as well as similarities. Diversity also can refer to a whole being made up of different parts. Diversity is often thought of as the condition of being **accepting** of all creeds and cultures and respectful of those **differences**. In the workplace, diversity can refer to the components of the employee population, which may include people of different ages, experience levels, and talent levels.

IMPACT OF DIVERSITY

The safety professional must be sensitive to the **different cultures, backgrounds, and experiences** of all employees. For example, some cultures respect authority to the degree that employees will not ask clarifying questions, even if they do not understand the information or expectations. Other groups may have been taught to work hard at the expense of their own safety, including long hours and risky behaviors. If the safety professional is not aware of the cultural differences within their workforce, this can lead to misunderstandings, bias, and accidents.

Understanding diversity means that trainings and other safety-related materials should be provided in the language that is **understood** by the employees. This may mean that handouts and warning signs are produced in multiple languages. Instructions may need to be visual, verbal, and hands-on to make sure that the literacy level of an employee does not impact the messaging. The goal of the safety professional is to provide a safe work environment for all employees.

BIAS

Bias refers to a conscious or unconscious **preference** for one thing over another. Bias can be interchanged with the term prejudice. Although prejudice and bias are often thought of as only negative, an individual can also have a prejudice or bias toward something. Bias and prejudice can interfere with **objectivity** and push a person to make a decision or draw a conclusion that may not be consistent with the facts. A positive bias toward a person may incline an individual to **believe** their side of a story more than another person's version. A negative bias toward a person or group may cause an individual to assign blame to the group that may not be warranted. Bias can also impact our **expectations**, either toward or against a person or group such that there is an unsupported expectation of success or failure. Professionals need to be aware that bias exists and work to avoid its impact on decisions.

IMPACT OF BIAS

An individual's bias can be against a group (employees in general, ethnic groups), an individual, or an organization. Safety professionals must consciously work to **eliminate** their biases by basing all incident investigations on facts and applying safety expectations evenly to everyone, regardless of their age, affiliation, or other identifying characteristic.

For example, if a safety professional has a negative opinion of a supervisor, an accident investigation report may place blame on the supervisor for an employee's poor decision. Similarly, if a safety officer has a pro-management bias, shortcomings in the safety management system are rarely cited as contributing factors, and workers seem to always be the cause of accidents. A safety professional should work

114

to avoid bias impacting their investigations, even if the results may not be seen as favorable by those who review the report.

STS Practice Test

Want to take this practice test in an online interactive format?
Check out the bonus page, which includes interactive practice
questions and much more:
https://www.mometrix.com/bonus948/sts

1. Which of the following excavation hazard control systems involves the use of wales, sheeting, and struts?

   A. Benching
   B. Sloping
   C. Shoring
   D. Ramping

2. Which of the following is the practice or aspect of including individuals with different backgrounds and experiences?

   A. Inclusivity
   B. Segregation
   C. Diversity
   D. Sensitivity

3. Which of the following must be considered for excavations that are deeper than five (5) feet?

   A. Electrocution from buried electrical lines
   B. Cave-ins
   C. Hazardous atmospheres from underground gas lines
   D. Equipment falling into a trench

4. In excavation/trenching work, the natural angle that soil forms when it is piled or collapses is known as the:

   A. Angle of tangential stability.
   B. Angle of recoil.
   C. Angle of lattice.
   D. Angle of repose.

5. According to OSHA, who is a competent person?

   A. The site safety officer, responsible for identifying hazards
   B. The most senior tradesman who is most familiar with procedure
   C. Someone authorized by an employer to correct and eliminate hazards
   D. A medical professional trained to identify and treat illnesses and injuries

6. An employee who was pressured by a supervisor to increase production output suffers a hand injury on the mechanical press they were using. A possible root cause of the injury could be:

    A. Worker distraction.

    B. Faulty interlock.

    C. Poor maintenance program.

    D. Improper PPE.

7. Which of the following is true of positioning device systems?

    A. These systems are required by OSHA to ensure support up to 100 pounds of gross weight.

    B. These systems are usually attached to lanyards or lifelines.

    C. Body harnesses or body belts are not parts of these systems.

    D. A worker is required to have one hand supporting and stabilizing the system during use.

8. Which of the following reduces the chances of a circuit acting as an ignition source?

    A. Installing insulators around transformer boxes

    B. Using LOTO devices

    C. Installing components subject to excessive resistance heating in climate-controlled areas

    D. Using short- to medium-length wiring

9. What is an interlock?

    A. An area in a decontamination zone

    B. A device that inhibits machine startup

    C. A LOTO device

    D. A device used to prevent access to a flammable cabinet

10. White finger syndrome results from excessive exposure to which of the following conditions?

    A. Excessive cold

    B. Excessive heat

    C. Vibrating tools

    D. Pinch points

11. Which of the following does NOT define a confined space?

    A. Has an access point that locks

    B. Is large enough to enter

    C. Has a limited means of entering

    D. Is not designed for continuous occupancy

12. What is the name of the system developed by the United Nations that specifies the requirements for hazardous materials labeling?

A. International Standards Organization
B. Globally Harmonized System
C. Occupational Health and Safety Administration
D. Occupational Health and Safety Assessment Series

13. In the field of ergonomics, what does the acronym "MSD" stand for?

A. Muscle system dysfunction
B. Multiple system dynamic
C. Musculoskeletal disorder
D. Material safety datasheet

14. According to OSHA, how soon after a fatal workplace accident occurs must it be reported?

A. As soon as possible after the occurrence
B. Within 8 hours of the occurrence
C. Within 24 hours of the occurrence
D. Within 72 hours of the occurrence

15. Which of the following would NOT be considered an engineering control?

A. HEPA filters
B. Ventilation dampers
C. Warning signs
D. Fire sprinklers

16. Which of the following is NOT part of an appropriate lockout/tagout (LOTO) procedure?

A. Using LOTO devices that are authorized for particular equipment or machinery and ensuring that the devices are durable, standardized, and substantial
B. Ensuring that new or overhauled equipment is capable of being locked out
C. Enforcing a policy that tagout devices may not be used without lockout devices under any circumstances
D. Inspecting and reviewing energy control documentation/protocols on at least an annual basis

17. Ordinary combustibles, such as paper and wood, are classified as what type of fuel?

A. Class B
B. Class K
C. Class C
D. Class A

18. According to OSHA, the use of _____ must be employed whenever a worker is performing tasks at least six (6) feet above a lower level.

    A. Ladders

    B. Fall protection equipment

    C. Headgear

    D. Slip-resistant footwear

19. To help reduce carbon monoxide accumulation in poorly ventilated warehouses, which of the following systems should internal combustion-powered industrial trucks use?

    A. Exhaust re-routers

    B. Organic HEPA stage inlets

    C. Catalytic converters

    D. Cabin filters

20. Which of the following heavy equipment safety devices reduce the risk of striking nearby workers?

    A. Seatbelts

    B. Backup alarms

    C. Rollover cages

    D. Headlights

21. Which of the following is a common root cause for injuries caused by manual hand tools?

    A. Using hand tools instead of power tools

    B. Using hand tools in wet environments

    C. Improper storage

    D. Improper maintenance

22. Which of the following types of electrical measures is most critical in worker injury or death due to electrocution?

    A. Voltage

    B. Current

    C. Conductivity

    D. Resistance

23. A-B-C-D-K applies to which of the following devices?

    A. Smoke detectors

    B. Automatic sprinkler systems

    C. Fire extinguishers

    D. Chemical spill kits

24. What is the most frequent cause of crane failure?

A. Improper assembly
B. Lack of an inspection program
C. Overloading
D. Striking stationary objects while moving a load

25. Always wearing required personal protective equipment; adhering to safety procedures; and equally enforcing safety policies to management, employees, and visitors is an example of:

A. Equity.
B. Anti-bias.
C. Leadership.
D. Integrity.

26. Which of the following is NOT a risk associated with occupational noise?

A. Inability to hear warning signals
B. Ear infection from improperly maintained hearing protection
C. Hearing loss
D. Stress

27. What is a corrective action?

A. A proactive measure to address hazards
B. A process to permanently address safety management system failures
C. A fix for the direct cause that led to an injury
D. A supervisor's report that is created in response to a safety inspection

28. The acronyms UFL, UEL, LFL, and LEL are commonly used by professionals when identifying which of the following?

A. Arcing potential for circuit panels
B. Boiling points for liquids
C. Melting points for solids
D. Ignitability levels for atmospheres

29. Which of the following is NOT a method used to control chronic exposure to a chemical?

A. Limit the amount of time a worker is exposed
B. Substitute a less hazardous substance
C. Install warning signs in the work area
D. Install local exhaust ventilation

30. Which of the following health effects are typically realized soon after exposure, disappear within a short period of time, and do not have long-lasting implications?

    A. Chronic
    B. Permanent
    C. Transient
    D. Acute

31. In fire codes, what term describes the intended usage of a building?

    A. Business class
    B. Fire rating
    C. Occupancy
    D. Permit class

32. Elevated temperature and humidity reduce the body's ability to cool itself and can result in:

    A. Accidents.
    B. Hypothermia.
    C. Hazard assessment.
    D. Heat illness.

33. The Occupational Safety and Health Act requires that employers provide _____ for their employees.

    A. Annual health checkups
    B. Insurance
    C. Uniforms
    D. Safety and health training

34. Below is a table of ambient noise levels within a work area measured over a 7-day period. From the data provided, which of the following conclusions should be drawn?

Measurement Day	Number of Hours Measured	Measurement Range	Measurement Average
1	8	74-81 dBA	77 dBA
2	6.25	67-79 dBA	71 dBA
3	5.5	86-88 dBA	87 dBA
4	7	71-92 dBA	79 dBA
5	8	81-85 dBA	84 dBA
6	6	77-80 dBA	78 dBA
7	6.75	58-72 dBA	67 dBA

    A. Mandatory hearing protection should always be worn in this work area.
    B. Mandatory hearing protection should be worn 25% of the time in this work area.
    C. Mandatory hearing protection should be worn 50% of the time in this work area.
    D. Mandatory hearing protection is not required in this work area.

35. Which of the following is NOT considered acceptable fall protection?
    A. Fall arrest systems (e.g., harnesses, lanyards)
    B. Roof and silo plugs
    C. Guardrails
    D. Safety nets

36. In a robust safety management system, the results of an audit should be provided to:
    A. Management, as only they can plan for corrective actions.
    B. Management and employees, in order to maintain transparency of the audit process.
    C. Employees, so they know how dangerous their workplace is.
    D. Supervisors, who can correct the hazards before management finds out.

37. What action should be taken when a safety non-conformance issue is identified?
    A. It should be brought up at the next scheduled safety committee meeting.
    B. The designated employee should document the incident and prepare a report for management.
    C. Work should stop immediately to correct the hazard.
    D. Work should stop at the next lunch break to correct the hazard.

38. Identify the term for a visual evaluation of safety equipment prior to use.
- A. Inspection
- B. Investigation
- C. Audit
- D. Hazard assessment

39. Which factor contributes most to poor indoor air quality in office environments?
- A. Noise
- B. Improper housekeeping
- C. Poor ventilation
- D. Odors

40. The coefficient of friction of a floor surface is used to assess slip risk. This coefficient falls within which of the following ranges?
- A. -1 to 1
- B. 1 to 100
- C. 0 to 1
- D. 1 to 10

41. The STS can best identify potential workplace hazards by:
- A. Conducting pre-job briefings.
- B. Holding plan of the day (POD) meetings.
- C. Conducting routine worksite inspections.
- D. Analyzing performance metrics.

42. What is the term used for two chemicals that, if mixed, can result in a violent reaction, toxic gas production, or explosion?
- A. Incoherent
- B. Inconsistent
- C. Incompatible
- D. Pyrophoric

43. Which of the following is the process used to proactively identify potential hazards associated with a job and correct them?
- A. Technical specification review
- B. Job hazard analysis
- C. Root cause analysis
- D. Lessons learned review

44. Which of the following is used to reduce or eliminate hazardous material exposure in the workplace?
- A. Gloveboxes
- B. Fire detection systems
- C. Personal protective equipment (PPE)
- D. Ventilation dampers

45. What is the difference between a corrective action and preventative action?

A. A corrective action corrects a problem that has occurred; a preventative action attempts to eliminate potential causes of a problem.

B. There is no difference; they are synonymous.

C. A corrective action addresses injuries; a preventative action addresses quality issues.

D. A corrective action is a negative reinforcement and a preventative action is a positive reinforcement.

46. A fall arrest system does which of the following?

A. Prevents employees from falling off an unprotected edge

B. Decelerates a falling employee before they strike the lower level

C. Covers a skylight to prevent an employee falling through the hole

D. Allows employees to work at heights using both hands

47. What are the two components of the fire tetrahedron that a fire safety program is designed to reduce or eliminate?

A. Oxygen and chain reaction

B. Oxygen and energy

C. Oxygen and fuel

D. Fuel and energy

48. What are an employer's responsibilities as they relate to fire protection systems?

A. Install and verify

B. Certify and upgrade the system as necessary

C. Inspect, maintain, and repair

D. None; upon installation, fire systems are approved until activated

49. What is the term for a person's strong adherence to their principles?

A. Integrity

B. Dedication

C. Loyalty

D. Morality

50. Which of the following is used to evaluate an emergency response and identify what worked well and what needs improvement?

A. Lessons learned

B. Root cause analysis

C. Hazard assessment

D. Emergency action plan

51. Identify the least effective method of preventing exposure to toxic welding fumes.

A. Employing an air-purifying respirator
B. Operating a local exhaust ventilation system
C. Using flux that is low in heavy metal content
D. Allowing welding to last for only two (2) hours per day

52. What is the purpose of wearing bright colors near heavy equipment?

A. Protection from the heat
B. Protection from rain
C. Increased ability to recognize who is allowed on site
D. Increased visibility

53. How often must insulated electrical gloves be tested?

A. Once each year
B. Quarterly
C. Twice each year
D. Monthly

54. Which of the following will an industrial hygienist use to identify potential inhalation hazards?

A. Audiometer
B. Air sampling
C. Anemometer
D. Calorimetry

55. Who is responsible for notifying BCSP regarding instances of a member violating the code of ethics?

A. Only clients who have been defrauded
B. The BCSP judiciary board
C. Any person who becomes aware of a violation
D. The BCSP credentialing board

56. Which of the following control methods found in NIOSH's hazard control hierarchy is the most effective at reducing risk?

A. Engineering
B. PPE
C. Elimination
D. Administrative

57. What is the most common mistake made when using ladders?

A. Exceeding the load limit on a ladder
B. Carrying tools while ascending or descending a ladder
C. Ladder manufacturing defects
D. Improper ladder selection

58. Which of the following systems presents a high-pressure hazard?

A. Boiler
B. Water line
C. Flammable chemical storage cabinet
D. Utility vault

59. Which of the following is the safest method to move compressed gas cylinders?

A. Using a cylinder cart
B. Rolling the cylinders on their edges
C. Using a sling
D. Rolling the cylinders horizontally

60. Which of the following is NOT a hazard associated with elevated work platforms?

A. Electrocution
B. Falls
C. Caught-between incident
D. UV radiation from welding

61. Which of the following is a component of the NIOSH lifting equation?

A. Slip coefficient (SC)
B. Recommended weight limit (RWL)
C. Axial leverage constant (ALC)
D. Load bearing (LB)

62. Which of the following is NOT a required component of an employer's emergency action plan?

A. Methods of reporting an emergency
B. Designated location for the written plan
C. Evacuation procedures
D. Accounting for employees after an evacuation

63. Which of the following can be defined as the act of motivating and directing people toward a common goal?

A. Leadership
B. Encouragement
C. Management
D. Punishment

64. Violating the BCSP Code of Ethics can result in which of the following?

A. Criminal proceedings
B. Civil action
C. Fine
D. Loss of credential

65. What glove material is used to protect the hands and arms during brazing and welding?

A. Denim
B. Rubber
C. Leather
D. Neoprene

66. Pinch point hazards are common for which of the following?

A. Table saws
B. Chains
C. Pulleys
D. Scaffolds

67. A safety professional who believes that employees are always at fault for an injury before the fact-collecting phase of an investigation has succumbed to:

A. Bias.
B. Prejudice.
C. Stereotyping.
D. Ethics violations.

68. Which class of fire extinguisher should be used to put out a fire inside of a 480V transformer?

A. Class A
B. Class B
C. Class C
D. Class E

69. Which of the following is a strategy that can be implemented in the pre-planning phase of a project to reduce the risk of a hazard?

A. Hiring contractors who are bonded and insured
B. Obtaining necessary permits
C. Assigning an appropriate number of employees to the project
D. Identifying material lay-down areas on the site map

70. Principles are _____ applicable beliefs.

A. Conditionally
B. Universally
C. Subjectively
D. Preferentially

71. Which of the following hazards is NOT commonly associated with poor housekeeping?

A. Rodents
B. Fire
C. Electrocution
D. Trips

72. In the general industry standards, what is the height above which fall protection measures are required?

A. 4 feet
B. 6 feet
C. 8 feet
D. 10 feet

73. What are the four elements of the fire tetrahedron?

A. Source, stoke, smoke, sustain
B. Oxygen, fuel, heat, chain reaction
C. Spark, combustion, oxygen, retention
D. Stop, drop, roll, extinguish

74. According to NIOSH, what is the leading cause of work-related fatalities?

A. Falls from heights
B. Electrocution
C. Motor vehicle accidents
D. Asphyxiation in confined spaces

75. For which of the following chemicals would butyl-rubber gloves NOT be necessary?

A. Hydrofluoric acid
B. Sodium hydroxide
C. Liquid iodine
D. Formic acid

76. Which of the following is true of OSHA inspection policies?

A. The employer may decline up to two OSHA inspections per year, provided that an adequate reason for rescheduling is submitted at least 30 days in advance.
B. The employer must have at least one senior level manager with the OSHA compliance officer at all times.
C. The OSHA compliance officer must notify the employer of an upcoming inspection 30 days prior to the visit.
D. The OSHA compliance officer must not reveal any trade secrets or proprietary information observed during an inspection.

77. What is the primary hazard associated with industrial lift vehicles?

   A. Striking pedestrians
   B. Dropping loads
   C. Carbon monoxide poisoning from the engine
   D. Falling/overturning

78. Which of the following would NOT be a risk factor to consider when using a mobile crane?

   A. Lack of natural light in work area
   B. Overloading the boom
   C. Improper rigging
   D. Presence of overhead electrical lines

79. What is the term for an organization's guiding set of principles that outlines the expected behavior for employees?

   A. Mission statement
   B. Code of ethics
   C. Vision statement
   D. Goals statement

80. When should a job hazard analysis (JHA) be updated?

   A. Never, as it is only required once
   B. Whenever a new employee is hired
   C. Periodically or after an injury
   D. When required by OSHA standards

81. Which of the following is NOT a component of the BCSP's Code of Ethics?

   A. Immediately issuing public statements to alleviate public concern
   B. Accepting assignments only when qualified with the appropriate education and experience for the task at hand
   C. Being responsible, honest, fair, and impartial
   D. Remaining unbiased about religion, ethnicity, gender, age, national origin, sexual orientation, and disability

82. Which of the following hazards are most commonly associated with heavy equipment at work sites?

   A. Dropped load
   B. Vibration
   C. Falling (such as off temporary roads)
   D. Struck-by

83. According to OSHA, which of the following is NOT considered a confined space requirement?

A. A space's ambient atmosphere shall always be tested for oxygen content levels prior to entry.

B. A determination shall be made whether the space requires a permit prior to entry.

C. Attendants are unnecessary if the entry is larger than a single person.

D. Appropriate signage designating the space as confined must always be posted.

84. What is the recommended frequency for conducting evacuation drills?

A. Monthly

B. Quarterly

C. Annually

D. Bi-annually

85. Which of the following sets of colors are used on the NFPA 704 diamond?

A. Green, black, gray, gold

B. Blue, orange, white, purple

C. Yellow, green, magenta, brown

D. Blue, red, yellow, white

86. What is the third and final step (after safety and isolation) that should be followed after a HAZMAT spill is detected?

A. Evacuation

B. Notification

C. Remediation

D. Inspection

87. Why is carbon dioxide an effective extinguishing agent for different fuel types?

A. Because humans exhale carbon dioxide, it is not toxic.

B. It is odorless, removes oxygen from a fire, and does not leave a residue.

C. It is lightweight and inexpensive.

D. When it deploys, it is cold and removes the heat energy from a fire.

88. What is the proper term for the program that is implemented to control hazardous energy in a system during maintenance or repair operations?

A. Blanking/blocking

B. Lockout/tagout (LOTO)

C. Energy isolation

D. Electrical safety program

89. Bias can be defined as:

A. Negative feelings toward a specific group.
B. A fact assumed to be true without proof.
C. A group of individuals sharing the same ideals.
D. An unconscious preference that impacts objective decision-making.

90. Which of the following is NOT a hazard associated with shielded metal arc welding (SMAW)?

A. Arc eye
B. Trigger finger
C. Toxic fumes
D. Burns

91. How does an employer ensure that employees are aware of the components of a fire safety plan, including the use of fire extinguishers and evacuation routes?

A. Having a written plan
B. Training and drills
C. Posting the requirements in a break room
D. Sending an email

92. Which of the following is most effective in reducing hazardous noise levels?

A. Limiting unprotected time in hazardous noise areas to no more than two hours a day
B. Isolating noise-generating equipment away from workers
C. Using a system that diverts background noise
D. Working in open environments to reduce echoing and reverberation

93. OSHA believes that a critical component of a health and safety program is:

A. Online resources.
B. Effective training.
C. Support from labor organizations.
D. Warning signs.

94. Which of the following is NOT a proper control method to reduce the risk of fire when storing fuel gas and oxygen welding cylinders?

A. Separating the fuel gas and oxygen cylinders by 20 feet
B. Storing the cylinders together in a room with a "no smoking" sign
C. Storing the cylinders in the same room, but separating them using a five-foot wall
D. Storing them in separate rooms

95. According to the Resource Conservation and Recovery Act (40 CFR Part 261), which of the following is a characteristic of hazardous waste with a specific waste code?

    A. Ignitability
    B. Silicosis
    C. Lead poisoning
    D. Carcinogenesis

96. Beverly is employed at a processing plant with poor machine guarding throughout. She often works near belts and pulleys, never tucks in her shirt, and always wears a long and dangling necklace. Which of the following types of accident would Beverly be most at risk for?

    A. Slip, trip, or fall
    B. Electrocution
    C. Caught-between
    D. Struck-by

97. Identify the program that is designed to reduce both the risk of fires from starting and also the spread of fires once they begin.

    A. Fire safety
    B. Fire suppression
    C. Life safety
    D. Emergency action plan

98. According to OSHA regulations, the air pressure limit for _____ shall not exceed 30 psi.

    A. Pneumatic drills
    B. Airbrushing
    C. Pneumatic jacks
    D. Compressed air for cleaning

99. A machine shop worker using a band saw while not wearing the required eye protection suffered a catastrophic eye injury from flying debris which resulted in the loss of that eye. The accident was reported to OSHA approximately 36 hours after the incident occurred. According to OSHA, the company:

    A. Is not required to report these types of incidents to OSHA, but is required to record them.
    B. Is in violation of the allowable 24-hour reporting time frame for this incident type.
    C. Is within the allowable reporting grace period of 48 hours.
    D. Should have delayed notifying OSHA for a period of at least 72 hours to ensure that the injury was permanent.

100. How can an employer reduce the risk of employee motor vehicle accidents?

    A. Installing global positioning devices

    B. Requiring defensive driver training

    C. Requiring eye exams for all employees who drive for work

    D. Instituting a policy prohibiting passengers in company vehicles

Answer Key and Explanations

1. C: In excavations, a shoring system is a cave-in prevention system that uses physical elements to support the soil. The system is comprised of poles, wales, sheeting, and struts that hold back the belly of the excavation to reduce the risk of failure. Shoring is typically used when there is inadequate space for sloping or benching.

2. C: Diversity is the practice of including individuals from different sub-groups into a larger collective. The sub-groups may share similar ethnicity, sexuality, economic status, or philosophy. Whereas inclusivity refers to equal access to resources and opportunities, diversity refers to having representation from multiple sub-groups.

3. B: OSHA has identified cave-ins as the highest risk for workers in trenches. Cave-ins can trap a worker and prevent them from exiting, which can result in suffocation. If a trench exceeds five (5) feet in depth, the employer must implement protective measures to prevent cave-ins.

4. D: The angle of repose is defined as the steepest angle that excavated soil can be piled without the material sliding or falling.

5. C: OSHA defines a competent person as an individual who recognizes hazards and is authorized to correct them. Typically, a competent person has advanced training, knowledge, or experience in a specific area, such as scaffolding, lifting sling inspection, and explosives storage.

6. A: Distractions divert workers' attention from the risks posed by the job they are performing. When workers are focused on increasing production and working quickly, they become less focused on working safely. This inattention to safe work practices may cause them to slip, place their hands in machinery power zones, bypass guard systems, or otherwise put themselves in a position to get injured.

7. B: Per 29 CFR 1910.140, positioning device systems are used in performing tasks that require one to use both hands on a vertical surface, such as elevated walls or window sills. Such systems consist of either a body harness or body belt and connectors.

8. D: The longer an electric wire is, the greater the resistance that is built up along the length of the wire, resulting in the wire increasing in temperature. This can create a potential ignition source in the presence of combustible materials. The use of short- to medium-length wiring helps mitigate this hazard.

9. B: A safety interlock is a device that inhibits a machine from operating when the device is interrupted. For example, a saw might have a guard that, when removed, will cut the power to the machine via the interlock so that the saw will shut down or not start.

10. C: White finger syndrome is the result of long-term exposure to vibrating hand tools. Vascular damage attributed to vibration exposure can result in blanching (a loss of color in the digits), numbness, loss of grip strength, and loss of dexterity.

11. A: 29 CFR 1910.146 identifies a confined space as any area that is large enough for an employee to enter, has limited or restricted means of entering, and is not designed for continuous human occupancy. Such spaces include tanks, silos, and vaults.

12. B: The United Nations has produced the Globally Harmonized System of Classification and Labeling of Chemicals, shortened to GHS. This system uses a series of standardized pictograms, hazard statements, and precautionary statements to convey chemical hazards to those who handle and use the substances. The GHS also standardizes the information provided in the safety datasheets across the globe to facilitate trade and the safe movement of hazardous materials between nations.

13. C: NIOSH uses the term "musculoskeletal disorder" (MSD) to refer to ergonomic injuries or disorders that occur to muscles, nerves, tendons, discs, joints, and cartilage. Such injuries or conditions are associated with long-term exposure to force, vibration, repetitive motion, and awkward positions, all of which are ergonomic injury risk factors.

14. B: OSHA 29 CFR 1904.39 requires that any work-related deaths must be reported within 8 hours.

15. C: Engineering controls are more effective than either administrative controls or PPE in that they remove or reduce a hazard. Examples of engineering controls include HEPA filters that capture hazardous particulates, dampers that can physically isolate a ventilation system, and fire suppression systems that automatically activate when a fire occurs. Warning signs are an administrative control because they attempt to influence behavior and are only effective if recognized and followed by employees, but do not address the hazard itself.

16. C: According to OSHA 1910.147, tagout devices are permitted for use in lieu of lockout devices under qualified circumstances.

17. D: Paper and wood are classified as ordinary combustibles. Thus, any suppression system rated for Class A fires, or combination fires including A, would be appropriate.

18. B: OSHA requires fall protection equipment (such as body harnesses, limit lines, or fall arrest systems) whenever a worker is 6 feet or more above the next lower level.

19. C: Catalytic converters are the best way to mitigate potential accumulation of carbon monoxide produced by internal combustion engines.

20. B: Backup alarms can be installed on heavy equipment to warn workers nearby that the equipment will be moving in a direction with limited visibility. The alarm must be loud enough for workers to hear over background noise or through hearing protection.

21. D: OHSA has determined that the greatest hazards from hand tools are caused by improper maintenance and improper use. Poor maintenance programs can allow tools with dull blades or cracked handles to be used until they fail, resulting in an injury. Dull cutting tools require additional effort by the worker, which can result in slipping or muscle injury.

22. B: The degree of injury associated with electrocution is directly linked to current. It does not require much current to kill. Current levels as low as 50 mA can affect the heart muscle, with current levels as low as 1.0 amps likely to result in death.

23. C: Fire extinguishers are classified using a letter and geometric shape system based on the type of fuel involved in a fire. Class A, represented by a green triangle, is for normal combustibles such as wood, paper, and plastic; Class B, indicated by a red square, is for combustible liquids such as gasoline, oil, and grease; Class C, symbolized by a blue circle, is for live electrical equipment; Class D, denoted by a yellow decagon, is for combustible metals such as sodium or potassium; and Class K, signified by a black hexagon, is for cooking oils and fats.

24. C: OSHA states that over 80% of cranes tipping or failing are a result of overloading. Overloading is when a crane or hoist is rigged to move more than its rated capacity. The structural stresses can cause the crane or hoist to fail and drop the load or tip over. Overloading can also be caused by dragging a load or when the load swings in windy conditions—both of which increase the stress on the structure.

25. C: Safety leadership is the quality of leading by example. Leadership is demonstrated by what the safety professional does and how they do it. The safety professional does not lead as if they are above the rules, but rather encourages others to follow by adhering to and enforcing the rules from the top down. Integrity, which is always doing the right thing, is a common quality of good leaders.

26. B: Elevated levels of noise in a worker's environment can have various health effects. Chronic exposure can lead to hearing loss at certain frequencies or ringing in the ears. When the brain is constantly bombarded with sound signals, the result may be physical or psychological stress. Noise can also impair an employee's ability to hear and respond to warning signals or alarms.

27. B: In a robust safety management system, a corrective action is a means to correct the system failure that is identified as the root cause of the injury during a post-accident investigation. Where a correction fixes the direct cause of an incident, a corrective action implements a system to prevent the incident from happening again. For example, if an injury is caused by an equipment failure due to low hydraulic fluid levels, a correction would be to simply replace the oil, but a corrective action would be to implement a routine maintenance program to monitor the fluid levels.

28. D: The acronyms for upper flammable limit (UFL), upper explosive limit (UEL), lower flammable limit (LFL), and lower explosive limit (LEL) all indicate the range at which a given flammable gas or vapor concentration would ignite. The difference between flammability limit and explosive limit is whether the fuel is confined where it could result in an explosion once ignited.

29. C: Chronic exposure is the result of working with a substance for an extended period of time, such as using paint thinner over an entire career. Chronic health effects are typically irreversible and show up later in life. To avoid chronic exposure, employers should evaluate using less hazardous substances, reduce the amount of time any worker uses a substance, or install ventilation to remove any vapors from being inhaled.

30. D: Acute health effects are those that usually manifest soon after exposure, typically remediate in a relatively short period of time, and likely do not result in permanent damage to organs. However, some chemicals are so toxic that even a short exposure can be fatal.

31. C: Occupancy is the term used in the fire codes to describe the intended usage of a building. For example, Group A is for assembly, such as convention halls. Group B is for business, including office spaces. Group H is for high hazard, such as a chemical storage room. And lastly, Group M is for mercantile, such as retail establishments. A building's occupancy type determines fire suppression system requirements, allowable storage limits for combustibles, and other elements of fire safety.

32. D: When the body is unable to reduce its internal temperature by normal mechanisms due to elevated temperatures, work rate, or humidity, the risk of heat illness increases. Heat illness, also known as hyperthermia, can result in dizziness, fainting, rashes, heat exhaustion, or even heat stroke in extreme cases.

33. D: The Occupational Safety and Health Act (1970) requires employers to provide safety and health training to all their employees, regardless of level, age, or experience. The Occupational Safety and Health Administration (OSHA) is responsible for enforcing this Act.

34. D: In examining the data, the work area does not have noise levels above 85 dBA averaged over 8 hours and therefore, per 29 CFR 1910.95, hearing protection is not mandatory.

35. B: According to OSHA 1910.28, fall arrest systems, guardrails, and safety nets are all acceptable for fall protection when a walking or working surface exceeds 4 feet above the next lower level.

36. B: A robust safety management system is designed to have vertical communication between all stakeholders. This means that audit results are provided to management so that they can develop plans and allocate resources, as well as to employees so that they are aware of hazards in the workplace. Open communication of audit results maintains the transparency and faith in the system.

37. C: Whenever a safety professional identifies a safety non-conformance, the work in the potentially impacted area should be stopped immediately to correct the hazard. No hazard should ever be left unmitigated if it can impact people, property, or the environment. A quick response to the situation will allow the project to safely move forward, but an accident investigation can halt operations for a much longer period of time.

38. A: An inspection is a visual evaluation of safety equipment that should be conducted at least once before every use. An inspection is used to identify worn, broken, or missing components of the system so that defective equipment does not introduce additional hazards into the workplace. Various OSHA standards require inspections before each use and at other frequencies, such as monthly or annually, depending on the standard. Equipment that requires inspections include respiratory protection, fall protection equipment, cranes, rigging, and chemical protective clothing.

39. C: OSHA has identified three primary factors that contribute to poor indoor air quality: temperature, humidity, and poor ventilation. High temperatures and humidity can promote the growth of mold in a facility, which can impact sensitive individuals. A proper HVAC system that introduces adequate outdoor air can circulate and filter the air while also moderating the temperature and humidity within a space.

40. C: The coefficient of friction range is between 0 and 1. A value less than 0.1 is very slippery and a value of 1 is non-slippery.

41. C: One of the most effective ways to identify potential workplace hazards is by conducting routine worksite inspections, audits, or evaluations.

42. C: Incompatible chemicals can mix to produce violent reactions (such as the flame caused by potassium metal contacting water), toxic gas production (formed when sodium cyanide mixes with an acid), or an explosion (when ammonia and chlorine gases combine). Therefore, all efforts must be made to store incompatible chemicals in separate locations from each other.

43. B: OSHA defines a job hazard analysis (JHA) as a technique to identify hazards associated with job tasks before an injury occurs. The JHA examines the interaction between the worker, the job, the environment, and the tools to identify potential risks, thereby allowing the employer to insert controls before work starts.

44. A: Effective tools for reducing or eliminating hazardous material exposures (i.e., chemical, radiological, biological) include gloveboxes, robotics, and physical

138

barriers. Personal protective equipment (PPE) is not a primary means of reducing hazardous material exposures.

45. A: Corrective and preventative actions (CAPA) are measures that are implemented once a root cause for an incident has been identified. Corrective actions are reactive and resolve safety management system conditions that resulted in an injury. A preventative action is a proactive measure to improve the safety system and prevent future injuries. The two are often grouped together under the "CAPA" abbreviation.

46. B: 29 CFR 1910.140 defines a personal fall arrest system as a system consisting of a body harness, anchorage, and connector "used to arrest [or stop] an employee in a fall from a walking-working surface." The connector consists of a deceleration device, lanyard, lifeline, or a combination of these.

47. D: A fire safety plan is designed to reduce or eliminate the fuel and energy components of the fire tetrahedron. By limiting the amount of combustible material present in any one location and separating flammable materials from other items, the fuel available to a fire is reduced. Addressing ignition sources by using non-sparking tools, installing intrinsically safe fixtures in fuel storage areas, and prohibiting smoking near fuel sources removes the energy needed to initiate a fire.

48. C: It is the responsibility of the employer to regularly inspect, maintain, and repair fire protection systems, including portable fire extinguishers and automatic suppression systems. The Fire Code outlines the inspection frequency for the various system components. An employer should hire certified contractors for any repairs or required recertifications due to the specialized nature of fire systems.

49. A: An individual who demonstrates a strong adherence to their principles is described as having integrity. Integrity can also be described as honesty and is applied evenly in all situations, without condition. Morality is the aspect of determining what is right or wrong. Thus, morality will guide integrity.

50. A: A lessons learned post-incident review is a method used to evaluate the efficacy of an emergency response plan. The review requires all stakeholders and participants to evaluate what elements functioned well and where there are areas for improvement. Areas identified for improvement can include the need for additional resources, including equipment or personnel, rewriting portions of the plan, or additional training.

51. A: An air-purifying respirator is a piece of personal protective equipment (PPE) used to control the exposure to toxic fumes. PPE is considered the least effective method to control a hazard because it does not address the hazard itself, but simply installs a barrier between the employee and the hazard and is dependent on proper use and selection to be effective. Preferred methods include eliminating the hazard by using low-toxicity flux, removing the hazardous fumes by ventilation, or a policy that reduces the time a worker is exposed to a hazard.

52. D: Heavy equipment presents a hazard as a result of obstructed visibility. Due to the size relative to the cab, location of the cab, or overall size of the vehicle, there is an increased risk of striking workers near the equipment. High visibility clothing increases the chance of the operator seeing and thereby avoiding collisions or impacts with workers in the area.

53. C: Per 29 CFR 1910.137, rubber insulating gloves used for protection against high voltage exposure must be tested twice each year.

54. B: Air sampling is the process of collecting a portion of air in a particular environment and subjecting it to laboratory analysis. The resultant information is used by an industrial hygienist to identify what, if any, controls are necessary to eliminate or reduce the chemicals that may be inhaled by the workers in that area.

55. C: Per the BCSP's disciplinary policy, any person who believes a certified member has violated the code of ethics may notify the chief executive officer. The complaint form is available on the BCSP website.

56. C: NIOSH identifies elimination as the most effective means of hazard control. If a hazard is removed from a work location, it no longer has the potential to cause an injury. Engineering controls isolate the hazard, but failure or removal of the control is still possible. Administrative controls require employees to adhere to the warnings and procedures. PPE is the least favorable option because it does nothing to mitigate the hazard, and any failure or improper use will result in an exposure.

57. D: According to the American Ladder Institute, one of the most common errors in ladder use is choosing the incorrect ladder. Using ladders that are too short or too long, choosing the wrong material of the ladder (wood, aluminum, or fiberglass), or using an A-frame ladder when an extension ladder should be used are all mistakes that increase the risk of injury.

58. A: Boilers and other systems that operate at high pressures present both impact and release hazards. Poor maintenance, improper installation, and human errors can result in failure of the system. If the system fails, the container may fragment, presenting a struck-by hazard. Additionally, the contents may present their own hazards, including burns from steam or exposure to the chemicals in the system, such as refrigerants.

59. A: A cylinder cart, specifically designed to securely and safely move cylinders, is the safest method to move compressed gas cylinders. Cylinders should be stored; secured; and moved vertically in the cart to prevent falling, which can damage the valve assembly.

60. D: Elevated work platforms, also referred to as aerial lifts, present a variety of hazards to the user. Whether electrocution by contact with overhead power lines, falling from the platform, or being pinned against an object while the lift is being raised (known as a caught-between incident), all potential hazards must be addressed before the lift is used. Additional hazards include falling objects, tip overs, and equipment failure.

61. B: When using the NIOSH lifting equation to determine the risk of manual materials handling, the resultant value is the recommended weight limit (RWL). This is calculated by evaluating the height of the load, the distance lifted, how far the load is from the body, any twisting involved, and the grip using a standard weight of 51 pounds. The RWL provides the maximum recommended weight for the lifting task being evaluated.

62. B: 29 CFR 1910.38 requires than an employer with more than 10 employees must have a written plan that outlines how employees are to report emergencies, how to evacuate and which exit routes are available, procedures for critical plant operations, a method to account for all employees after evacuation, any requirements for employees performing medical or rescue duties, and contact information for employees looking for additional information.

63. A: Leadership is the act of motivating and directing people toward a common goal. For a safety professional, that involves influencing employees to achieve organizational safety goals by demonstrating and encouraging safe behaviors.

64. D: The Board of Certified Safety Professionals has adopted a disciplinary policy that states a member may lose their credential if they violate the adopted BCSP Code of Ethics. The formal proceeding includes a hearing by the judicial commission and, if a violation is deemed to have occurred, the individual may have their credential permanently revoked.

65. C: Gloves made from leather are used for protection when welding or brazing. They are durable against abrasion, protect from sparks and metal slag, and are resistant to sharp edges.

66. C: Pinch point hazards are associated with moving machinery, particularly those which rotate toward each other or toward a fixed point. They can trap body parts, hair, dangling jewelry, or clothing. Examples of equipment that have pinch point hazards include pulleys, gears, belts, bearings, and rollers. Limiting employee proximity to these types of equipment through installing guarding is the most effective method for protecting against this hazard.

67. A: Bias can be defined as a tendency to hold a belief against a particular group. In this case, the bias is against employees by believing that they are the cause of accidents. This bias does not take into consideration the culpability of management, who may not provide adequate training or equipment and may not support a culture of safety.

68. C: Class C extinguishers are rated for use on electrical fires. They contain chemicals that do not conduct electricity and still disrupt the fire tetrahedron (heat, oxygen, fuel, chain reaction). By coating the area with a non-conductive dry chemical, the fire is deprived of oxygen, thus extinguishing it.

69. D: The pre-planning stage of any project is an opportunity to mitigate potential hazards by implementing controls before the work begins. Such mitigation strategies can include identifying drop-off points for materials to reduce the opportunities for vehicle-worker interaction. Additionally, strategic placement of materials can reduce the amount of movement required, which can reduce the risk of injuries due to falling materials and lifting, as well as the need for additional equipment to move materials from storage areas to the work areas.

70. B: Principles are defined as beliefs that are universally applicable and not bound by groups, cultures, or individuals. The principles of fairness, honesty, and integrity are considered right regardless of an individual's origin or environment. To differentiate, ethics are specific to a group and are enforced by the group, while morals are specific to an individual.

71. C: Poor housekeeping is the term used for the improper management of scrap, debris, materials, and tools. When clutter is present, it can provide refuge and food supplies for pests, including rodents and insects. Upon ignition, debris, scrap, trash, and stored materials all provide a fuel source that can allow a fire to propagate quickly and sustain itself. Debris and tools in walkways can also present tripping hazards, resulting in fall-related abrasions, contusions, and fractures.

72. A: 29 CFR 1910.28 requires that fall protection systems be implemented when the distance between an unprotected edge or side is more than four (4) feet above the next lower level.

73. B: The fire tetrahedron includes four elements: fuel, oxygen, heat, and chain reaction. Removal of any one of these elements will inhibit or stop a fire.

74. C: Between 1992 and 2001, motor vehicle accidents were the leading cause of death on the job. During that span, nearly 22% of all occupational fatalities were attributed to motor vehicle accidents.

75. C: Butyl rubber gloves are used for handling corrosive materials like strong acids (e.g., hydrofluoric, formic, hydrochloric, sulfuric, nitric) and strong bases (e.g., sodium hydroxide, potassium hydroxide). Liquid iodine has a more neutral pH and can therefore be safely handled with nitrile gloves.

76. D: OSHA inspectors must not reveal any trade secrets seen during the inspection. A representative of the employer must accompany the inspector, but they do not need to be senior management level. OSHA inspectors are not required to give notice prior to their visit, though they do need to present official identification when they arrive and they must always reveal and make known the reason for the inspection.

77. D: According to the National Institute of Occupational Safety and Health (NIOSH), the primary hazard associated with industrial lift vehicles, such as forklifts, is the vehicle falling off the loading dock or overturning and crushing an employee.

78. A: According to NIOSH, the leading cause of mobile cranes getting tipped over is when the load exceeds the lift capacity of the unit. Additionally, dropped loads from improper rigging and contact with overhead electrical lines are common causes of crane-related injuries.

79. B: A code of ethics, such as that for the Board of Certified Safety Professionals, is an organization's set of principles that guides the conduct and expected behavior of its members. Members of the group use the code of ethics to assist them in making decisions related to activities when representing the group.

80. C: A job hazard analysis (JHA) should be conducted for each task in a workplace. Periodically updating the JHA is recommended to ensure it is still relevant and to identify any hazards that may have been missed during the initial analysis. Additionally, whenever there has been an injury, the JHA should be reviewed to determine whether procedures or equipment need to be changed to lower the risk. OSHA standards do not designate the frequency of conducting a JHA.

81. A: The BCSP's Code of Ethics includes the following principles: accepting assignments only when one is qualified by an appropriate combination of education and experience in specific technical fields; conducting oneself honestly, fairly, impartially, and with responsibility and integrity; acting in a manner free of bias with regard to religion, ethnicity, gender, age, national origin, sexual orientation, or disability; maintaining as top priority the safety and health of people, the protection of the environment, and protection of property in the performance of professional duties; avoiding deceptive acts that falsify or misrepresent academic or professional qualifications; conducting professional relations via the highest standards of integrity and avoiding compromise of professional judgment with potential conflicts of interest; seeking opportunities to be of constructive service in civic affairs and working for the advancement of safety, health, and wellbeing of the community and profession; and issuing public statements only in an objective and truthful manner when founded upon knowledge of the facts and competency in a particular subject matter area.

82. D: Heavy equipment operators work with very large moving vehicles that have obstructed views. They typically do not have a complete field of vision around the vehicle. Thus, the operator has blind spots that can put nearby workers at risk of being struck, either by the vehicle or by the load being managed by the equipment. Additionally, heavy equipment can strike other equipment, materials, or structures while moving.

83. C: According to OSHA 1910.146, a confined space's atmosphere shall always be tested for oxygen levels prior to entry ($19.5\% \leq O_2 \leq 23.5\%$), a determination shall be made whether the space qualifies under the permit program, and appropriate signage designating the space as confined must always be posted. The use of outside attendants is always mandatory, regardless of the number of entry points or their size.

84. C: Unless otherwise stated in NFPA 101- Life Safety Code, annual evacuation drills are typically considered adequate to meet the stated standard of familiarizing employees with evacuation procedures. Some occupancies and businesses may require more frequent drills.

85. D: The four colors of the NFPA 704 diamond are red, white, yellow, and blue. Each color represents a hazard presented by chemicals stored at a location. Red at the top of the diamond indicates flammability, white at the bottom indicates special hazards such as oxidizers, yellow on the right side indicates chemical reactivity, and blue on the left indicates health hazards. The level of hazard is indicated using numbers ranging from 0 to 4, with 0 being the lowest and 4 being the highest.

86. B: The three-step process that should be used in the event of a hazardous material(s) spill is (1) safety of those near the spill, (2) containment/isolation, and (3) notification.

87. B: Carbon dioxide (CO_2) is a colorless, odorless gas. When deployed, it suffocates a fire by displacing the oxygen, thereby interrupting the fire tetrahedron. Unlike dry chemical agents, CO_2 does not leave a residue and is not corrosive, which is preferred when used near electronic equipment. Thus, CO_2 can be used on ordinary combustibles, flammable fluids, and electrical fires. However, CO_2 extinguishers are heavy and, if used in small spaces, can create a hazardous atmosphere.

88. B: 29 CFR 1910.147 uses the term lockout/tagout (LOTO) as the means of controlling hazardous energy. Hazardous energy includes electricity, high-pressure fluids and gases, and also gravity (such as a lift or press) and springs. The system uses a lock and tag system to prevent another employee from energizing the system during maintenance or repair.

89. D: Bias can be defined as an unconscious preference that impacts decision-making. These preferences may cause the individual to ignore objective evidence and arrive at an unsubstantiated decision. Bias can impact root cause determination in accidents, leading a safety professional to misidentify the direct cause. Safety professionals must understand that bias exists and actively work to remove it from their decision-making.

90. B: Common hazards associated with shielded metal arc welding include burns, electric shock, toxic metal fume inhalation, particulate inhalation, and arc eye (which is caused by corneal swelling from overexposure to UV light).

91. B: Employers are required to conduct training and drills for the elements of their fire safety plan. Employers should conduct evacuation drills so that employees know what to do and where to go in an emergency. Practicing using or handling fire extinguishers increases an employee's comfort with the device, which can be helpful if usage is ever required.

92. B: Isolating workers away from noisy equipment is an effective engineering control to reduce or eliminate hazardous noise exposure.

93. B: The Occupational Safety and Health Administration believes that training is an essential component of a health and safety program. Training should be effective to ensure that employees can recognize the hazards they face on the job, as well as how to avoid injury from those hazards.

94. B: Per 29 CFR 1910.253, stored fuel gas cylinders, including those for welding, must be separated from oxygen cylinders by at least 20 feet or using a 5-foot wall with a fire rating of at least 30 minutes. This can include storing the cylinders in separate rooms.

95. A: According to 40 CFR 261, ignitability (code #D001) is a category for characteristic hazardous waste. The other coded categories include corrosivity (code #D002), reactivity (code #D003), and toxicity (codes #D004 through #D043).

96. C: Because she works around multiple pinch points and carries risks associated with them (untucked shirt, long necklace), a caught-between type of accident from a pinch point is most likely. Caught-between injuries can result in injury (up to and including amputation) or death.

97. A: A fire safety program describes the systems, practices, and equipment that are used to reduce both the risk of fire and the spread and resultant losses from a fire. The program includes fire suppression equipment, emergency response actions, proper storage for flammable materials, training, and regular inspections.

98. D: According to OSHA 29 CFR 1910.242, compressed air used for cleaning shall be limited to 30 psi.

99. B: According to OSHA 29 CFR 1904.39, loss of an eye, amputation, or hospitalization must be reported within 24 hours. Failure to appropriately report can result in a violation and potential fiscal penalty.

100. B: Motor vehicle accidents are a leading cause of workplace fatalities. Employers can require employees to undergo defensive driving courses to reduce the frequency of accidents. Defensive driving is when a vehicle operator anticipates road hazards and takes measures to avoid them in a proactive manner.

How to Overcome Test Anxiety

Just the thought of taking a test is enough to make most people a little nervous. A test is an important event that can have a long-term impact on your future, so it's important to take it seriously and it's natural to feel anxious about performing well. But just because anxiety is normal, that doesn't mean that it's helpful in test taking, or that you should simply accept it as part of your life. Anxiety can have a variety of effects. These effects can be mild, like making you feel slightly nervous, or severe, like blocking your ability to focus or remember even a simple detail.

If you experience test anxiety—whether severe or mild—it's important to know how to beat it. To discover this, first you need to understand what causes test anxiety.

Causes of Test Anxiety

While we often think of anxiety as an uncontrollable emotional state, it can actually be caused by simple, practical things. One of the most common causes of test anxiety is that a person does not feel adequately prepared for their test. This feeling can be the result of many different issues such as poor study habits or lack of organization, but the most common culprit is time management. Starting to study too late, failing to organize your study time to cover all of the material, or being distracted while you study will mean that you're not well prepared for the test. This may lead to cramming the night before, which will cause you to be physically and mentally exhausted for the test. Poor time management also contributes to feelings of stress, fear, and hopelessness as you realize you are not well prepared but don't know what to do about it.

Other times, test anxiety is not related to your preparation for the test but comes from unresolved fear. This may be a past failure on a test, or poor performance on tests in general. It may come from comparing yourself to others who seem to be performing better or from the stress of living up to expectations. Anxiety may be driven by fears of the future—how failure on this test would affect your educational and career goals. These fears are often completely irrational, but they can still negatively impact your test performance.

> **Review Video: 3 Reasons You Have Test Anxiety**
> Visit mometrix.com/academy and enter code: 428468

Elements of Test Anxiety

As mentioned earlier, test anxiety is considered to be an emotional state, but it has physical and mental components as well. Sometimes you may not even realize that you are suffering from test anxiety until you notice the physical symptoms. These can include trembling hands, rapid heartbeat, sweating, nausea, and tense muscles. Extreme anxiety may lead to fainting or vomiting. Obviously, any of these symptoms can have a negative impact on testing. It is important to recognize them as soon as they begin to occur so that you can address the problem before it damages your performance.

> **Review Video: 3 Ways to Tell You Have Test Anxiety**
> Visit mometrix.com/academy and enter code: 927847

The mental components of test anxiety include trouble focusing and inability to remember learned information. During a test, your mind is on high alert, which can help you recall information and stay focused for an extended period of time. However, anxiety interferes with your mind's natural processes, causing you to blank out, even on the questions you know well. The strain of testing during anxiety makes it difficult to stay focused, especially on a test that may take several hours. Extreme anxiety can take a huge mental toll, making it difficult not only to recall test information but even to understand the test questions or pull your thoughts together.

> **Review Video: How Test Anxiety Affects Memory**
> Visit mometrix.com/academy and enter code: 609003

Effects of Test Anxiety

Test anxiety is like a disease—if left untreated, it will get progressively worse. Anxiety leads to poor performance, and this reinforces the feelings of fear and failure, which in turn lead to poor performances on subsequent tests. It can grow from a mild nervousness to a crippling condition. If allowed to progress, test anxiety can have a big impact on your schooling, and consequently on your future.

Test anxiety can spread to other parts of your life. Anxiety on tests can become anxiety in any stressful situation, and blanking on a test can turn into panicking in a job situation. But fortunately, you don't have to let anxiety rule your testing and determine your grades. There are a number of relatively simple steps you can take to move past anxiety and function normally on a test and in the rest of life.

> **Review Video: How Test Anxiety Impacts Your Grades**
> Visit mometrix.com/academy and enter code: 939819

Physical Steps for Beating Test Anxiety

While test anxiety is a serious problem, the good news is that it can be overcome. It doesn't have to control your ability to think and remember information. While it may take time, you can begin taking steps today to beat anxiety.

Just as your first hint that you may be struggling with anxiety comes from the physical symptoms, the first step to treating it is also physical. Rest is crucial for having a clear, strong mind. If you are tired, it is much easier to give in to anxiety. But if you establish good sleep habits, your body and mind will be ready to perform optimally, without the strain of exhaustion. Additionally, sleeping well helps you to retain information better, so you're more likely to recall the answers when you see the test questions.

Getting good sleep means more than going to bed on time. It's important to allow your brain time to relax. Take study breaks from time to time so it doesn't get overworked, and don't study right before bed. Take time to rest your mind before trying to rest your body, or you may find it difficult to fall asleep.

> **Review Video: The Importance of Sleep for Your Brain**
> Visit mometrix.com/academy and enter code: 319338

Along with sleep, other aspects of physical health are important in preparing for a test. Good nutrition is vital for good brain function. Sugary foods and drinks may give a burst of energy but this burst is followed by a crash, both physically and emotionally. Instead, fuel your body with protein and vitamin-rich foods.

Also, drink plenty of water. Dehydration can lead to headaches and exhaustion, especially if your brain is already under stress from the rigors of the test. Particularly if your test is a long one, drink water during the breaks. And if possible, take an energy-boosting snack to eat between sections.

> **Review Video: How Diet Can Affect your Mood**
> Visit mometrix.com/academy and enter code: 624317

Along with sleep and diet, a third important part of physical health is exercise. Maintaining a steady workout schedule is helpful, but even taking 5-minute study breaks to walk can help get your blood pumping faster and clear your head. Exercise also releases endorphins, which contribute to a positive feeling and can help combat test anxiety.

When you nurture your physical health, you are also contributing to your mental health. If your body is healthy, your mind is much more likely to be healthy as well. So take time to rest, nourish your body with healthy food and water, and get moving as much as possible. Taking these physical steps will make you stronger and more able to take the mental steps necessary to overcome test anxiety.

Mental Steps for Beating Test Anxiety

Working on the mental side of test anxiety can be more challenging, but as with the physical side, there are clear steps you can take to overcome it. As mentioned earlier, test anxiety often stems from lack of preparation, so the obvious solution is to prepare for the test. Effective studying may be the most important weapon you have for beating test anxiety, but you can and should employ several other mental tools to combat fear.

First, boost your confidence by reminding yourself of past success—tests or projects that you aced. If you're putting as much effort into preparing for this test as you did for those, there's no reason you should expect to fail here. Work hard to prepare; then trust your preparation.

Second, surround yourself with encouraging people. It can be helpful to find a study group, but be sure that the people you're around will encourage a positive attitude. If you spend time with others who are anxious or cynical, this will only contribute to your own anxiety. Look for others who are motivated to study hard from a desire to succeed, not from a fear of failure.

Third, reward yourself. A test is physically and mentally tiring, even without anxiety, and it can be helpful to have something to look forward to. Plan an activity following the test, regardless of the outcome, such as going to a movie or getting ice cream.

When you are taking the test, if you find yourself beginning to feel anxious, remind yourself that you know the material. Visualize successfully completing the test. Then take a few deep, relaxing breaths and return to it. Work through the questions carefully but with confidence, knowing that you are capable of succeeding.

Developing a healthy mental approach to test taking will also aid in other areas of life. Test anxiety affects more than just the actual test—it can be damaging to your mental health and even contribute to depression. It's important to beat test anxiety before it becomes a problem for more than testing.

> **Review Video: Test Anxiety and Depression**
> Visit mometrix.com/academy and enter code: 904704

Study Strategy

Being prepared for the test is necessary to combat anxiety, but what does being prepared look like? You may study for hours on end and still not feel prepared. What you need is a strategy for test prep. The next few pages outline our recommended steps to help you plan out and conquer the challenge of preparation.

STEP 1: SCOPE OUT THE TEST

Learn everything you can about the format (multiple choice, essay, etc.) and what will be on the test. Gather any study materials, course outlines, or sample exams that may be available. Not only will this help you to prepare, but knowing what to expect can help to alleviate test anxiety.

STEP 2: MAP OUT THE MATERIAL

Look through the textbook or study guide and make note of how many chapters or sections it has. Then divide these over the time you have. For example, if a book has 15 chapters and you have five days to study, you need to cover three chapters each day. Even better, if you have the time, leave an extra day at the end for overall review after you have gone through the material in depth.

If time is limited, you may need to prioritize the material. Look through it and make note of which sections you think you already have a good grasp on, and which need review. While you are studying, skim quickly through the familiar sections and take more time on the challenging parts. Write out your plan so you don't get lost as you go. Having a written plan also helps you feel more in control of the study, so anxiety is less likely to arise from feeling overwhelmed at the amount to cover.

STEP 3: GATHER YOUR TOOLS

Decide what study method works best for you. Do you prefer to highlight in the book as you study and then go back over the highlighted portions? Or do you type out notes of the important information? Or is it helpful to make flashcards that you can carry with you? Assemble the pens, index cards, highlighters, post-it notes, and any other materials you may need so you won't be distracted by getting up to find things while you study.

If you're having a hard time retaining the information or organizing your notes, experiment with different methods. For example, try color-coding by subject with colored pens, highlighters, or post-it notes. If you learn better by hearing, try recording yourself reading your notes so you can listen while in the car, working out, or simply sitting at your desk. Ask a friend to quiz you from your flashcards, or try teaching someone the material to solidify it in your mind.

STEP 4: CREATE YOUR ENVIRONMENT

It's important to avoid distractions while you study. This includes both the obvious distractions like visitors and the subtle distractions like an uncomfortable chair (or a too-comfortable couch that makes you want to fall asleep). Set up the best study environment possible: good lighting and a comfortable work area. If background music helps you focus, you may want to turn it on, but otherwise keep the room quiet. If you are using a computer to take notes, be sure you don't have any other windows open, especially applications like social media, games, or anything else that could distract you. Silence your phone and turn off notifications. Be sure to keep water close by so you stay hydrated while you study (but avoid unhealthy drinks and snacks).

Also, take into account the best time of day to study. Are you freshest first thing in the morning? Try to set aside some time then to work through the material. Is your mind clearer in the afternoon or evening? Schedule your study session then. Another method is to study at the same time of day that you will take the test, so that your brain gets used to working on the material at that time and will be ready to focus at test time.

STEP 5: STUDY!

Once you have done all the study preparation, it's time to settle into the actual studying. Sit down, take a few moments to settle your mind so you can focus, and begin to follow your study plan. Don't give in to distractions or let yourself procrastinate. This is your time to prepare so you'll be ready to fearlessly approach the test. Make the most of the time and stay focused.

Of course, you don't want to burn out. If you study too long you may find that you're not retaining the information very well. Take regular study breaks. For example, taking five minutes out of every hour to walk briskly, breathing deeply and swinging your arms, can help your mind stay fresh.

As you get to the end of each chapter or section, it's a good idea to do a quick review. Remind yourself of what you learned and work on any difficult parts. When you feel that you've mastered the material, move on to the next part. At the end of your study session, briefly skim through your notes again.

But while review is helpful, cramming last minute is NOT. If at all possible, work ahead so that you won't need to fit all your study into the last day. Cramming overloads your brain with more information than it can process and retain, and your tired mind may struggle to recall even previously learned information when it is overwhelmed with last-minute study. Also, the urgent nature of cramming and the stress placed on your brain contribute to anxiety. You'll be more likely to go to the test feeling unprepared and having trouble thinking clearly.

So don't cram, and don't stay up late before the test, even just to review your notes at a leisurely pace. Your brain needs rest more than it needs to go over the information again. In fact, plan to finish your studies by noon or early afternoon the day before the test. Give your brain the rest of the day to relax or focus on other things, and get a good night's sleep. Then you will be fresh for the test and better able to recall what you've studied.

STEP 6: TAKE A PRACTICE TEST

Many courses offer sample tests, either online or in the study materials. This is an excellent resource to check whether you have mastered the material, as well as to prepare for the test format and environment.

Check the test format ahead of time: the number of questions, the type (multiple choice, free response, etc.), and the time limit. Then create a plan for working through them. For example, if you have 30 minutes to take a 60-question test, your limit is 30 seconds per question. Spend less time on the questions you know well so that you can take more time on the difficult ones.

If you have time to take several practice tests, take the first one open book, with no time limit. Work through the questions at your own pace and make sure you fully understand them. Gradually work up to taking a test under test conditions: sit at a desk with all study materials put away and set a timer. Pace yourself to make sure you finish the test with time to spare and go back to check your answers if you have time.

After each test, check your answers. On the questions you missed, be sure you understand why you missed them. Did you misread the question (tests can use tricky wording)? Did you forget the information? Or was it something you hadn't learned? Go back and study any shaky areas that the practice tests reveal.

Taking these tests not only helps with your grade, but also aids in combating test anxiety. If you're already used to the test conditions, you're less likely to worry about it, and working through tests until you're scoring well gives you a confidence boost. Go through the practice tests until you feel comfortable, and then you can go into the test knowing that you're ready for it.

Test Tips

On test day, you should be confident, knowing that you've prepared well and are ready to answer the questions. But aside from preparation, there are several test day strategies you can employ to maximize your performance.

First, as stated before, get a good night's sleep the night before the test (and for several nights before that, if possible). Go into the test with a fresh, alert mind rather than staying up late to study.

Try not to change too much about your normal routine on the day of the test. It's important to eat a nutritious breakfast, but if you normally don't eat breakfast at all, consider eating just a protein bar. If you're a coffee drinker, go ahead and have your normal coffee. Just make sure you time it so that the caffeine doesn't wear off right in the middle of your test. Avoid sugary beverages, and drink enough water to stay hydrated but not so much that you need a restroom break 10 minutes into the test. If your test isn't first thing in the morning, consider going for a walk or doing a light workout before the test to get your blood flowing.

Allow yourself enough time to get ready, and leave for the test with plenty of time to spare so you won't have the anxiety of scrambling to arrive in time. Another reason to be early is to select a good seat. It's helpful to sit away from doors and windows, which can be distracting. Find a good seat, get out your supplies, and settle your mind before the test begins.

When the test begins, start by going over the instructions carefully, even if you already know what to expect. Make sure you avoid any careless mistakes by following the directions.

Then begin working through the questions, pacing yourself as you've practiced. If you're not sure on an answer, don't spend too much time on it, and don't let it shake your confidence. Either skip it and come back later, or eliminate as many wrong answers as possible and guess among the remaining ones. Don't dwell on these questions as you continue—put them out of your mind and focus on what lies ahead.

Be sure to read all of the answer choices, even if you're sure the first one is the right answer. Sometimes you'll find a better one if you keep reading. But don't second-guess yourself if you do immediately know the answer. Your gut instinct is usually right. Don't let test anxiety rob you of the information you know.

If you have time at the end of the test (and if the test format allows), go back and review your answers. Be cautious about changing any, since your first instinct tends to be correct, but make sure you didn't misread any of the questions or accidentally mark the wrong answer choice. Look over any you skipped and make an educated guess.

At the end, leave the test feeling confident. You've done your best, so don't waste time worrying about your performance or wishing you could change anything. Instead, celebrate the successful completion of this test. And finally, use this test to learn how to deal with anxiety even better next time.

> **Review Video: 5 Tips to Beat Test Anxiety**
> Visit mometrix.com/academy and enter code: 570656

Important Qualification

Not all anxiety is created equal. If your test anxiety is causing major issues in your life beyond the classroom or testing center, or if you are experiencing troubling physical symptoms related to your anxiety, it may be a sign of a serious physiological or psychological condition. If this sounds like your situation, we strongly encourage you to seek professional help.

Thank You

We at Mometrix would like to extend our heartfelt thanks to you, our friend and patron, for allowing us to play a part in your journey. It is a privilege to serve people from all walks of life who are unified in their commitment to building the best future they can for themselves.

The preparation you devote to these important testing milestones may be the most valuable educational opportunity you have for making a real difference in your life. We encourage you to put your heart into it—that feeling of succeeding, overcoming, and yes, conquering will be well worth the hours you've invested.

We want to hear your story, your struggles and your successes, and if you see any opportunities for us to improve our materials so we can help others even more effectively in the future, please share that with us as well. **The team at Mometrix would be absolutely thrilled to hear from you!** So please, send us an email (support@mometrix.com) and let's stay in touch.

> **If you'd like some additional help, check out these other resources we offer for your exam:**
> **http://MometrixFlashcards.com/STS**

Additional Bonus Material

Due to our efforts to try to keep this book to a manageable length, we've created a link that will give you access to all of your additional bonus material:

mometrix.com/bonus948/sts